The Qur'ān and the Prophet in the Writings of Shaykh Aḥmad al-ʿAlawī

OTHER TITLES ON THE SHAYKH AL-ʿALAWĪ
PUBLISHED BY THE ISLAMIC TEXTS SOCIETY

A Sufi Saint of the Twentieth Century:
Shaikh Aḥmad al-ʿAlawī His Spiritual Heritage and Legacy

OTHER TRANSLATIONS OF SUFI TITLES

A Collection of Sufi Rules of Conduct

The Key to Salvation

The Secret of Secrets

The Speech of the Birds

The Way of Abū Madyan

The Qur'ān and the Prophet in the Writings of Shaykh Aḥmad al-ʿAlawī

Translated by Khalid Williams

ISLAMIC TEXTS SOCIETY

This first edition published 2013 by
The Islamic Texts Society
Miller's House
Kings Mill Lane
Great Shelford
Cambridge CB22 5EN, UK.

British Library Cataloguing-in-Publication Data.
A catalogue record for this book is
available from the British Library.

ISBN: 978 1903682 760 cloth
ISBN: 978 1903682 777 paper

Arabic calligraphy in Appendix II by
arabiccalligraphy4u.com

Contents

PREFACE

Shaykh Muṣṭafā Aḥmad al-ʿAlawī, also known as Bin ʿAlīwā, was the spiritual pole of his age and one of the greatest Sufis of the past few centuries and in fact of the whole history of Sufism. He was attracted early in his life to various Sufi orders in his home country of Algeria and finally after meeting Shaykh Būzīdī joined the Darqāwiyyah Branch of the Shādhiliyyah Order. The spiritual gifts of Shaykh al-ʿAlawī soon became manifest. He became a spiritual master himself and his spiritual eminence and *barakah* caused numerous disciples to join his circle which had its center in Mostaghanem in northern Algeria where he resided. Soon his fame spread not only throughout Algeria and the Maghrib in general, but to other parts of the Islamic world and even in certain circles in the West. He established his own branch of the Shādhiliyyah-Darqāwiyyah Order which came to be known as the ʿAlawiyyah Order, an order that began to spread rapidly not only in the Maghrib, but also in Yemen, Syria and other lands east as far as Indonesia. When he died in 1934, he had thousands upon thousands of disciples all over the Islamic world, guided by his spiritual functionaries, some of whom became themselves famous spiritual masters such as Shaykh al-Hāshimī and Shaykh ʿAbd al-Q̱ādir in Syria. After the death of Shaykh al-ʿAlawī, Shaykh ʿAddah bin Tūnis succeeded him in Mostaghanem, which continued as the mother *zāwiyah* of the Order in the Maghrib while other branches of the Order continued to function, mostly independently, in other lands. The ʿAlawiyyah Order survives to this day as a major Sufi order with numerous disciples in both the Islamic world and the West.

Shaykh al-ʿAlawī was a true universalist and esoterist and it was he who was chosen by Heaven to fulfil the prediction of Shaykh al-Shādhilī that one day the light of his *Ṭarīqah* would shine upon the West. It is especially significant in relation to this prediction that it was Shaykh al-ʿAlawī who was invited by the French government to inaugurate in 1927 the beautiful Paris mosque which was constructed in a completely traditional manner by Muslim architects and craftsmen from North Africa in the Maghribī style. He accepted the invitation and delivered the first *khuṭbah* in that precious mosque. To this day his *barakah* is present in this sacred space that stands miraculously in the middle of a completely non-Islamic ambience in a major Western city.

This event symbolizes the beginning of the spread of the *barakah* of the Shādhiliyyah Order in the West, but the real spread of the Order itself in Europe came when one of Shaykh al-ʿAlawī's rare European disciples who had been initiated by him in Mostaghanem, that is, Shaykh ʿĪsā Nūr al-Dīn Aḥmad, whose Western name was Frithjof Schuon, returned to Europe in 1932 and soon thereafter began a European branch of the ʿAlawiyyah Order. As Shaykh ʿĪsā once told us, it was a momentous task to open the Western cosmic ambience to the possibility of the presence of authentic Sufism, but nevertheless the task was accomplished and the prediction of Shaykh al-Shādhilī realized seven centuries after him. It is important to note that all the authentic Sufi orders such as the Qādiriyyah and Naqshbandiyyah as well as other branches of the Shādhiliyyah Order, which have a serious presence in the West today, established themselves there after Shaykh al-ʿAlawī's disciple Shaykh ʿĪsā had succeeded in sinking the roots of the Shādhiliyyah-ʿAlawiyyah Order into the 'soil' of the Western world which had been Christian but had now become to a large extent post-Christian.

Shaykh al-ʿAlawī was a supreme metaphysician and saint but he was also a major Islamic scholar. While his main task was to train human souls and expound the deepest truths of *al-maʿrifah* or gnosis, he was also engaged in those social and intellectual debates of the day that concerned the integrity of the Islamic tradition. To this end he combated both modernism and the rise of anti-Sufi and anti-metaphysical Salafism that was spreading into the Algeria of his day from eastern Arab lands. Like his spiritual heritage, his intellectual *jihād* in this domain is still of the utmost significance today when the integral message of traditional Islam, which includes teachings about both the Law (*al-Sharīʿah*) and the Way (*al-Ṭarīqah*) and at the heart of which stands the Truth (*al-Ḥaqīqah*), is being threatened by both modernism and so-called fundamentalism that is grounded in a truncated and impoverished understanding of the Islamic message.

The heritage of Shaykh al-ʿAlawī includes not only the ʿAlawiyyah Order but also a large corpus of works in both prose and poetry. These books continue to be reprinted in the original Arabic while many of them have also been translated into French and a few into other European and Islamic languages. There are not, however, many translations into English. Knowledge of Shaykh al-ʿAlawī began to spread in the English speaking world through the masterly work of Martin Lings, that is, Shaykh Abū Bakr Sirāj al-Dīn, who himself belonged to Shaykh al-ʿAlawī's spiritual lineage. This work, entitled *A Sufi Saint of the Twentieth Century*, contains many precise and elegant translations of selections from Shaykh al-ʿAlawī's prose works as well as exquisite renderings of some of his Arabic poems into English poetry. After over half a century since its apparition this work remains the most pertinent and profound study in English on Shaykh al-ʿAlawī, read widely by many and translated into other European languages including French as well as the major Islamic languages such as Arabic, Persian and Turkish. But despite its wide dissemination, Lings' book did not lead to extensive translation of Shaykh al-ʿAlawī's works into English in contrast to French into which many of his works have been rendered during the past several decades mostly through the efforts of the ʿAlawiyyah Order itself. As far as English is concerned, the only translation of note of

Shaykh al-ᶜAlawī that appeared after the book of Lings was that of Leslie Cadavid in her *Two Who Attained*.

The present work by Khalid Williams—who also belongs to the spiritual lineage of Shaykh al-ᶜAlawī—is therefore a precious addition to the small corpus of the works of the sage of Mostaghanem available in the English language. In a both scholarly and spiritually authentic manner, Khalid Williams has selected, translated and analyzed some of the most important writings of the Shaykh on the twin sources of the Islamic tradition, namely, the Qur'ān and Ḥadīth, including a section devoted to responses to questions posed to him in relation to these twin sources. During his life time, Shaykh al-ᶜAlawī was often asked to write a commentary on the Noble Qur'ān. He did not respond by writing a commentary on the whole text but he did compose a commentary on several *sūrahs* which are included in this book. These works reveal him to be a master Sufi commentator of Islam's Sacred Scripture in the tradition of the classical Sufi commentators such as Imam al-Qushayrī, Ibn ᶜArabī, ᶜAbd al-Razzāq al-Kāshānī, Ibn Barrajān, Ibn ᶜAjība and the like but with many 'new' insights. His commentaries on the Ḥadīth also follow the long tradition of esoteric commentaries on the Prophetic traditions written by Sufis over the ages.

Khalid Williams is to be congratulated for producing a work that makes available for the first time in English so many of the basic writings of Shaykh al-ᶜAlawī on the basis of sources of the Islamic tradition. His choice of what was to be translated, his careful translation of the Arabic texts and his analyses are all to be commended. The result is a book that reveals Shaykh al-ᶜAlawī's method of commentary, his mastery as a commentator, his exposition of esoteric knowledge, his authority as a spiritual master and the universality of his vision. This work is therefore a major contribution to Islamic and Sufi studies in general and to Shādhilī and Maghribī Sufism in particular. But this book does not speak to these matters alone. It also bears a most precious and timely spiritual and intellectual message of universal import for all people in search of the truth, be they Muslim or non-Muslim. I hope and pray that this work receives the extensive attention that it deserves.

wa'Llāh^{u} aʿlam^{u} bi'l-ṣawāb

Seyyed Hossein Nasr
March 2013 A.D.
1434 A.H.

TRANSLATOR'S INTRODUCTION

Shaykh Aḥmad al-ʿAlawī was one of the most famous Sufi saints of the last century, with many followers both in the Muslim world and in Europe. Dr Martin Lings's bestselling biography of the Shaykh al-ʿAlawī, *A Sufi Saint of the Twentieth Century: Shaikh Aḥmad al-ʿAlawī his spiritual heritage and legacy*,[1] brought him to the attention of the English-reading public. The Shaykh was a prolific author and his works covered several traditional Islamic subjects including jurisprudence, doctrine and, of course, Sufism. But of this literary heritage nothing exists in English aside from the selections which were translated by Dr Lings in *A Sufi Saint* and Leslie Cadavid's book *Two Who Attained: Twentieth Century Sufi Saints: Shaykh Ahmad al-Alawi and Fatima al-Yashrutiyya*[2] which includes translations of some selections from his mystical commentary on the Mālikī legal text *al-Murshid al-muʿīn*.

Throughout his life, the Shaykh al-ʿAlawī was drawn to the exegesis (*tafsīr*) of the Qur'ān, and his teachings on the subject have been preserved both in his treatises and in records of answers he gave to his disciples in his regular gatherings. This book presents for the first time in English all the collected works of the Shaykh on the two guiding principles of Islam: the Qur'ān and the Prophet.

I do not intend to give a detailed biography of the Shaykh here; a thorough account of his life as told by the Shaykh himself can be found in Dr Lings's book. What follows is a brief outline of his life.

1 Martin Lings, *A Sufi Saint of the Twentieth Century: Shaikh Aḥmad al-ʿAlawī his spiritual heritage and legacy* (Cambridge: Islamic Texts Society, 1993).

2 Leslie Cadavid, *Two Who Attained: Twentieth Century Sufi Saints: Shaykh Ahmad al-Alawi and Fatima al-Yashrutiyya* (Louisville: Fons Vitae, 2005).

Shaykh Aḥmad al-ʿAlawī was born in 1869 in Mostaghanem, Algeria. In his early adulthood he was associated with the ʿĪsāwiyya, a Sufi order originating in Meknes, Morocco, and popular in the Islamic Maghreb. The order was then, and remains to this day, famous for the unusual antics of its followers such as fire-eating, snake-charming and the like. The Shaykh discovered that he had a natural talent for snake-charming, but in the end found that his spiritual aspiration was not satisfied by these practices and that his vocation lay elsewhere. It was then that he met Shaykh Ḥāmū al-Būzīdī who, unimpressed with his display of snake-charming, challenged him to charm a snake 'bigger than this and far more venomous: your soul, which is between the two sides of your body.'[1] The Shaykh al-ʿAlawī became al-Būzīdī's disciple in the Shādhilī-Darqāwī order and kept his company for some fifteen years. Upon al-Būzīdī's death in 1909 without nominating a successor, various visions and premonitions of the other disciples led them to believe that the Shaykh al-ʿAlawī should succeed him. At first, his order remained a branch of the broader Darqāwī brotherhood, but in 1914, after making himself independent of the mother *zāwiya* in Morocco, he named his order the Shādhiliyya-Darqāwiyya-ʿAlawiyya.

The Shaykh remained settled in Mostaghanem until the end of his life, but travelled extensively. As well as making the pilgrimage to Mecca and Medina, he visited Syria, the seat of the Caliphate in Istanbul, and also made a trip France, where he delivered the inaugural address at the Great Mosque in Paris. His fame spread throughout Algeria[2] and beyond, and many came to visit him to receive initiation, in addition to those who received it from him during his travels. In this way, his order spread far and wide during his lifetime, reaching even as far as Great Britain, where Yemeni disciples formed a *zāwiya* in Cardiff.

1 Lings, *ASufi Saint*, p. 52.
2 A shaykh of the ʿAlawī order in Morocco told me that by the time of the Shaykh al-ʿAlawī's death, there was not a single town, village or hamlet in Algeria that did not have an ʿAlawī presence.

The Shaykh also oversaw the publication of two newspapers that were distributed throughout Algeria by his disciples; they were meant to preach the teachings of traditional Islam to the general population in order to counter both the growth of Western-style secularism and the spread of the fundamentalist Wahhābī sect of Islam.

In addition to holding gatherings of teaching and invocation in the *zāwiya* in Mostaghanem, the Shaykh al-ʿAlawī authored works on several fields of Islamic scholarship and a large volume of poetry; some of these works were published in his lifetime and others after his death.[1] Some of the Shaykh's oral teachings were also collected by his disciples and published at the order's own printing press in Mostaghanem; which continues to operate to this day.

Shaykh Aḥmad al-ʿAlawī passed away in 1934 in Mostaghanem and was buried in the mother *zāwiya*. He was succeeded by his disciple Shaykh ʿAdda Bin Tūnis in Mostaghanem, as well as by various independent shaykhs in the Muslim world and also in the West.

For the present work, the decision was made to concentrate on the Shaykh's teachings, both written and oral, on the two most important sources of Islamic knowledge: the Qur'ān and the Prophet. Despite their being the most important references for all Muslims, there are surprisingly few English translations of Qur'ānic exegesis, particularly those of a Sufi bent, and hardly anything at all on the spiritual nature and qualities of the Prophet. For this reason it seemed apt to collect the works of the Shaykh al-ʿAlawī on these themes and gather them in a single volume. Let us now introduce each of these in turn:

1) From *The Swelling Sea: An Exegesis of the Qur'ān by Pure Light* (al-Baḥr al-masjūr fī tafsīr al-Qur*'ān bi-maḥḍ* al-nūr)[2]: the Author's Introduction, Commentary on the *Basmala* and Commentary on the 'Opening of the Book.'

As he mentions in his introduction to *The Swelling Ṣea*, the Shaykh received several requests from his disciples to produce an exegesis of

1 For a complete list of the Shaykh's writings, see Lings, *A Sufi Saint*, pp. 230-231.
2 Mostaghanem: al-Maṭbaʿa al-ʿAlāwiyya, 1995.

the entire Qur'ān. This he never did, although he began in earnest the work *al-Baḥr al-masjūr fī tafsīr al-Qur'ān bi-maḥḍ al-nūr*, intended to be a complete exegesis of the Qur'ān, each verse treated to four different levels of interpretation: the exegetical (*al-tafsīr*, meaning the literal meaning of the text and its historical background), the juridical[1] (*istinbāṭ al-aḥkām*), the allegorical (*al-ishāra*) and finally the purely spiritual (*lisān al-rūḥ*, 'the tongue of the Spirit'). This may be compared to the view of St Thomas Aquinas that scripture may be interpreted on four distinct levels: the historical, the aetiological, the analogical and the allegorical.[2] Regarding his four levels of interpretation, the Shaykh says: 'It occurred to me to arrange it by first mentioning the exegesis, that is, the general meaning of the Book of God; and then to mention any rulings that might be derived from it, which is a deeper level; and then to provide any allegory that might be derived from it, according to the language of the Folk of God; and finally to speak on an even deeper level, by means of the tongue of the Spirit. These are four rivers, as you can see, and *all people know their drinking-place* [Q.II.6].'[3]

The Shaykh stressed in his introduction that the Qur'ān must be seen as a living revelation, constantly offering new wonders to those who seek them; and that although some verses have historical significance, they are not limited to this, but are personally relevant to everyone who reads them: 'The most important thing we can do when reading the Book of God is to consider that it is being transmitted to us right now from the divine Presence.'[4]

But this work was never completed, and after reaching as far as verse 106 of the second Chapter (*al-Baqara*), the Shaykh discontinued the work because, as he said: '...I took to writing down what my inward thoughts dictated to me by way of interpretation of the Book of God, and I was so much under its sway that I brought them out in a

1 The Shaykh includes both legal and doctrinal matters in this category.
2 John Hood (ed.), *The Essential Aquinas: Writings on Philosophy, Religion, and Society* (Westport: Praeger, 2002), p. 168.
3 *The Swelling Sea*, p. 30.
4 *Ibid.*, p. 27.

strange and abstruse form. This is what led me to begin my commentary on *al-Murshid al-muᶜīn*,[1] in an attempt to stop myself from falling into a still more abstruse manner of expression.'[2]

Of this unfinished work, here are translated the Shaykh's introduction, his commentary on the *Basmala* formula ('In the Name of God, the Compassionate, the Merciful') which heads every Chapter of the Qur'ān save for one, and his commentary on the *Sūrat al-Fātiḥa* (Q.I). The commentary on the *Sūrat al-Baqara* (Q.II), being unfinished, has not been included here.

In examining the *Basmala*, the Shaykh discourses on the identity of the Name with the Named, the mysterious presence of God in all things, and the way in which the *basmala* symbolises the whole of the Qur'ān.

The Shaykh's commentary on the *Fātiḥa* shows a great deal of interest in the form of the Chapter: the word order, word choices, and pronoun shifts. He draws from this the concept, perhaps unique in *tafsīr* literature, that there is a hierarchical descent of the divine Presence in the Chapter, mirroring the hierarchy of the world of manifestation: first there is God alone as Subject and Object, then God as the Object of human consciousness, then God as the guide and giver of grace; then the focus shifts to those who follow the path to God, then those who incur God's wrath, and then finally those who are astray. God's presence in the *Fātiḥa* goes from the open to the hidden, from the *ẓāhir* to the *bāṭin*, from 'He,' to 'You,' to 'other than You.'

2) *The Kernel of Knowledge on the Chapter of the Star* (Lubāb al-ᶜilm fī Sūrat wa'l-Najm).[3]

Despite the discontinuation of the larger work, the Shaykh continued to receive requests for Qur'ānic exegesis, and in 1915

1 Selections of this commentary, entitled *al-Minaḥ al-Quddūsiyya*, 'The Divine Graces', may be found in Lings, *A Sufi Saint of the Twentieth century*, from which this quotation is taken, and also Leslie Cadavid, *Two Who Attained: Twentieth Century Sufi Saints: Shaykh Ahmad al-Alawi and Fatima al-Yashrutiyya* (Louisville: Fons Vitae, 2005).

2 Lings, *A Sufi Saint*, p. 58.

3 Mostaghanem: al-Maṭbaᶜa al-ᶜAlāwiyya, n.d.

he produced a commentary on Chapter LIII, *Sūrat al-Najm*. The Shaykh chose this Chapter because of the personal affinity he felt for it; as he said elsewhere, 'whosoever reflects upon this Chapter might almost fall down in prostration even before he reaches its final verse.'[1]

This work did not follow the pattern of the discontinued commentary, with its four levels of interpretation, but rather more closely resembles the aforementioned *Divine Graces* in that it interpreted the Chapter, not according to its literal or historical meaning, but rather as a symbol of the Sufi 'wayfarer' (*sā'ir*) on his journey to God. Thus those who *follow naught but surmise, and what the souls desire* (Q.LIII.23) are not, as would usually be understood, those who deny the existence of God, or who worship idols; in the perspective which the Shaykh al-ʿAlawī adopts in this work, they are rather those believers who cannot or will not accept what he calls 'pure Unity' (*al-tawḥīd al-maḥḍ*), the affirmation of belonging to God alone and to no other. According to this interpretation, this is nothing other than the 'Oneness of Being' of which the Sufis speak,[2] and the Shaykh's exegesis of the second half of the Chapter is centred on this doctrine and the path which the Sufi follows to reach full experiential realization of it.

As for the first half of the Chapter, it is concerned with the events of the Prophet's Ascension (*miʿrāj*) to the heavens.[3] The Shaykh al-ʿAlawī focuses on a single element of the Ascension, that of the moment when the Prophet drew *but two bows' nigh, or*

1 See Appendix I.

2 The term *waḥdat al-wujūd* is generally not found in the Shaykh al-ʿAlawī's works; he preferred *waḥdat al-shuhūd*, the 'Oneness of Vision', but it is clear from his writings that his understanding of being is identical to that of Ibn ʿArabī and the other proponents of *waḥdat al-wujūd*, rather than that of Sirhindī and his rival theory of *waḥdat al-shuhūd*. See Lings, *A Sufi Saint*, chapter five. For Sirhindī's understanding of *waḥdat al-shuhūd*, see William Chittick, *The Sufi Path of Knowledge: Ibn al-ʿArabi's Metaphysics of Imagination* (Albany: SUNY Press, 1989), p. 226.

3 See Martin Lings, *Muhammad: his life based on the earliest sources* (Cambridge: Islamic Texts Society, 1994), chapter 32.

nearer (Q.LIII.9) to God and, according to many exegetes and virtually all Sufis, partook of the beatific Vision. The Shaykh takes the opportunity to speak at length about this Vision, not only as it applied to the Prophet but as it may apply to all gnostics, and in doing so he puts forth some interpretations which are uncommon to say the least, but dazzling in their insight. For one, he takes the verses: *And He grew clear to view, when He was on the uppermost horizon; then He drew nigh, and came down* (Q.LIII.6–8) to refer to God, not the angel Gabriel, as the commentators usually opine, which provokes a deep and subtle metaphysical explanation of the way in which God 'comes down' to the gnostics even as they 'go up' to God.[1] Thus the Ascension is not only a historical account of an experience unique to the Prophet, but a symbol of the process whereby all saints ascend to God and attain to experiential knowledge of Him—save that 'their *miʿrāj* is only spiritual while that of the Prophet was also bodily.'[2]

Secondly, this subject inspires the Shaykh to quote some of the most difficult passages from the Gospel of John—which would present a problem to most Muslim scholars—and to find in them a support for his own perspective. This was a distinctive quality of the Shaykh al-ʿAlawī: he was not fazed by any religious statement but was always able to relate it to his own perspective, no matter how seemingly foreign it might seem to be to the Muslim view of things. Thus, the words of Christ, 'I and the Father are one' (John 10:30), which most Muslims, exoterists and esoterists alike, would most probably dismiss as a forgery, are for the Shaykh al-ʿAlawī a perfectly valid expression of the 'pure Unity' in which he is interested—albeit an expression which requires 'interpretation and commentary, just as some of the statements of the gnostics require

1 'The divine Love saves by making Itself what we are; it descends in order to elevate.' Frithjof Schuon, *Understanding Islam* (Bloomington: World Wisdom, 1998), p. 191.
2 Seyyed Hossein Nasr, *The Garden of Truth* (New York: Harper Collins, 2007), p. 123.

the same.' Yet despite their possible danger, the Shaykh cannot accept that statements such as these be rejected by way of erring on the side of caution, for 'to reject them would be even worse, for they are not without wisdom which the wise can understand.' As for whether or not they are truly the words of Christ in a historical sense, this does not interest the Shaykh as long as there is something to be gained from them, and it is enough for him to precede his comments with the qualification 'If these words are truly the words of Christ...,' and then to proceed with his explanation of them.

We see this same boldness and unshakeable composure when it comes to the Shaykh al-ʿAlawī's explanation of the story of the so-called 'Satanic Verses,'[1] where again he does not concern himself with an examination of the historical soundness of the story, but simply offers his explanation of it as though it were true, since either way it presents no problem to him.

Concerning once more the latter part of Chapter LIII, we see that the Shaykh sees, in the verses concerning the Prophet's efforts to preach to the people and their subsequent rejection of him, a symbol of the spiritual guide (*murshid*) in his efforts to lead his disciples along the path to God—*the uttermost end* (Q.LIII.42). The one who *turns away* (Q.LIII.33) means the one who traverses the path for a while, and then is distracted or obstructed by a delusion or vain fancy—the *surmise* of which the Chapter speaks. For those disciples who are able to avoid these obstacles, the *uttermost end* of the path to which the guide leads them is 'annihilation in God' (*al-fanā' fī 'Llāh*), which the Shaykh sees manifested in the final verses of the Chapter (Q. LIII.43–53). For the Shaykh, this symbolizes the extinction of the Sufi in his Lord, wherein all things disappear and only God remains; if God whelmed all these actions in His own action, and if He destroyed all those towns and people, then 'this is what He does with all creation in the eyes of the gnostic when He shows His magnificence to him.' Nothing remains but God.

1 See Appendix I.

3) *The Key to Mystical Knowledge in the Commentary on the Chapter 'Time'* (Miftāḥ ʿulūm al-sirr fī tafsīr Sūrat al-ʿAṣr).[1]

In later years, the Shaykh also composed a short commentary on Chapter CIII of the Qur'ān (*Sūrat al-ʿAṣr*), of which Martin Lings says: 'Whereas most commentators take the words *Verily man is in a state of ruin* [Q.CIII.2] to refer to the degeneracy of the pre-Islamic Arabs, Persians and others, [the Shaykh al-ʿAlawī] takes them to refer to the state of bodily man on earth as compared with his purely spiritual state in Heaven after he was 'created' (*makhlūq*) but before he was 'formed' (*muṣawwar*).'[2]

In his commentary on this Chapter, the Shaykh al-ʿAlawī examines the mysterious identity between God and time, inspired by the famous *ḥadīth* which states that 'God is Time.' The word *ʿaṣr* can mean 'afternoon', 'era' or 'time.' The Shaykh al-ʿAlawī's commentary focuses on the meaning 'time', in particular its divine connotations, hence our rendering of it as 'Time' here."

4) *The Outspreading Tree of Mysteries On the Meaning of the Invocation of Blessings on the Chosen Prophet* (Dawḥat al-asrār fī maʿnā al-ṣalāt ʿalā al-nabī al-mukhtār).[3]

Finally, included in this collection is the treatise *The Outspreading Tree of Mysteries On the Meaning of the Invocation of Blessings on the Chosen Prophet*, the Shaykh al-ʿAlawī's commentary on the Darqāwī master Muḥammad b. al-Ḥabīb's invocation of blessings on the Prophet entitled *Kanz al-ḥaqā'iq* 'The Treasury of Truths'. In the course of the commentary, the Shaykh expounds on the meaning of *ṣalāt* (blessing) and *salām* (peace), and their respective correspondence to the Sufi terms *fanā'* (extinction) and *baqā'* (subsistence), drunkenness and sobriety, and how the perfected saint requires a balance of the two. He also speaks about the Sufi concept of the 'Muḥammadan Light,' offering in

1 Mostaghanem: al-Maṭbaʿa al-ʿAlāwiyya, n.d.
2 Lings, *Sufi Saint*, p. 231.
3 Mostaghanem: al-Maṭbaʿa al-ʿAlāwiyya, 1991.

the course of doing so a mystical interpretation of the 'Verse of Light' (Q.XXIV.35).

5) Appendix I: The Shaykh al-ᶜAlawī's Answers to Questions on Qur'ān and Ḥadīth: Selections from *The Freshest Spring: Answers and Letters* (Aᶜdhab al-manāhil fī al-ajwiba wa'l-rasā'il).[1]
In Appendix I are translated answers given by the Shaykh al-ᶜAlawī to questions put to him by his disciples on the subjects of the Qur'ān and Ḥadīth; they are taken from the book *Aᶜdhab al-manāhil fī al-ajwiba wa'l-rasā'il*, a collection of such answers, and also letters written by the Shaykh on various topics. The collection includes answers given on such diverse matters as jurisprudence, doctrine, exegesis, politics, and history; from this have been selected for translation here only those sections pertaining to the Qur'ān and Ḥadīth.

Note on the Translation of Qur'ānic Verses

Martin Lings' unfinished *The Holy Qur'ān: Translations of Selected Verses*[2] has been followed wherever a translation for the required verse existed; otherwise, I relied mostly on the translations of A. J. Arberry, Marmaduke Pickthall and M. A. S. Abdel Haleem. Quotations from the Bible follow the Authorized Version, with slight modifications.

1 Mostaghanem: al-Maṭbaᶜa al-ᶜAlāwiyya, 1993.
2 Cambridge: Royal Aal al-Bayt Institute for Islamic Thought and Islamic Texts Society, 2007.

Shaykh al-ʿAlawī's Introduction to *The Swelling Sea: An Exegesis of the Qur'ān by Pure Light*[1]

In the Name of the God, the Compassionate, the Merciful

May blessings and peace be upon the Holy
Prophet and his Family and Companions

Praise be to God, who sent down the Book to His servant, whom He chose from all His creatures, *in a clear Arabic tongue* [Q.xxvi.195], *a clarification of all things* [Q.xvi.89] and a guide and mercy for the righteous; a Qur'ān *which guides to rightness, and we believe in it* [Q.lxxii.2], and to this we testify. I praise Him (Exalted and Glorious is He) and give thanks to Him for not making our understanding of His Word subject to the understanding of those who came before us. The Qur'ān is far too glorious to be confined to the understanding of anyone in all the worlds; for if it were, then it would be addressed solely to that person, and not to all mankind. It is *a Book whose verses are set clear* [Q.xi.1]; *to admonish all who are alive, and that the word may bear witness against those who believe not* [Q.xxxvi.70]. It will always remain fresh and new in every era, and is not worn out by the passage of time or repeated recitation. Even now it is, as it were, being delivered by the Trusted Spirit (*al-rūḥ al-amīn*),[2] or we might say even by the Most Merciful Himself. This

1 *Al-Baḥr al-masjūr fī tafsīr al-Qur'ān bi-maḥḍ al-nūr*. Mostaghanem: al-Maṭbaʿa al-ʿAlāwiyya, 1995, pp. 11-32.
2 The angel Gabriel; reference to Q.xxvi.192-193: *The Trusted Spirit brought it down to your heart.*

is what we believe about the Book of God, and I have no doubt whatsoever about it.

I testify that there is no god but God, the testimony of those who have knowledge of Him; and I testify that He is One and Unique in his Essence, Qualities and Acts. He is Outwardly Manifest in His Dominion, and Inwardly Hidden in His Essence. He *sent His Messenger with guidance and the religion of Truth, that He may make it prevail over all religion* [Q.IX.33]—our master Muḥammad, may God bless him his Family, Companions, and all his wives and progeny and those who came after them, following and supporting the religion; and may He grant them all abundant and goodly peace—peace which covers us as well as them.

Aḥmad ibn Muṣṭafā al-ʿAlawī, acknowledging his many sins and shortcomings in the sight of his Lord, says: When I resolved to set down in writing my understanding of the Book of God, I imagined that someone might say, 'The sages of old did not leave anything left to be said!' I therefore decided to begin my work with an introduction reminding the reader that all grace is in the hand of God, and cannot be held back by anyone. I elected to call my understanding of the Book of God *The Swelling Sea: An Exegesis of the Qur'ān by Pure Light*.[1] I hope that it will live up to its name; and there can be no power or strength save through God.

AN IMPORTANT NOTE: The reader should not begin this exegesis without passing through its sections in their proper order, as they are like a ladder leading up to its secrets. The reader should strive wherever possible to give the benefit of the doubt, and not to compare what he finds in this book with his own personal opinions, since they are unlikely to correspond. This is because the discourse of the Spirit is not like the discourse of the body, and most of what is in this book came to us on the tongue of special inspiration (*lisān al-khuṣūṣiyya*), which we have by no means mastered; all we have is what has been

1 *Al-Baḥr al-masjūr fī tafsīr al-Qur'ān bi-maḥḍ al-nūr*.

granted us from the Divine Presence. What this means is that this book is the product of neither arduous effort, nor random musing. I do not absolve myself of shortcomings, nor do I ignore the good that has been granted me. *God is aware of all that you do* [Q.II.234].

Now it occurred to me to arrange the work by first mentioning the exegesis (*tafsīr*), that is, the general meaning of the Book of God; and then to mention any rulings (*aḥkām*) that might be derived from it, which is a deeper level; and then to provide any allegory (*ishārāt*) according to the language of the Folk of God (*ahl Allāh*)[1]; and finally to speak on an even deeper level, by means of the tongue of the Spirit (*lisān al-rūḥ*).[2] These are four rivers, as you can see, and *all people know their drinking-place* [Q.II.60].

Prologue Explaining Six Key Points

Point One: upholders of the truth exist at all times.

Pertaining to what we have said above, Ibn ʿAbd al-Barr[3] and other eminent scholars (may God be pleased with them) have said when relating the words of their predecessors, 'Nothing is more dangerous for knowledge, scholars and students than the claim that the scholars of old have not left anything to be said by those who came after them.' Indeed this is so, for such a claim would make a dead letter out of many noble souls and sound intellects—God is our sufficiency, and the best of patrons! Yet the one who makes or believes such a claim has no basis for it other than his poor opinion of the remaining righteous of the believers (*al-bāqiyāt al-ṣāliḥāt*)[4]. Because of this, I searched the traditions for something more worthy of consideration. Far be it for God to leave His Beloved's community wandering in bewilderment;

1 That is, the Sufis.
2 These levels have been indicated in the text by the labels 'exegetical', 'juridical', 'allegorical' and 'spiritual.'
3 The Mālikī jurist of Andalusia (d. 1071).
4 This phrase is used twice in the Qur'ān (XVIII.46 and XIX.76) and is usually interpreted to mean good deeds which endure forever; the Shaykh's Arabic readers would not miss the reference.

it remains a community which upholds the truth and does justice in its light. If we only maintained a good opinion of the Muḥammadan community, this would be sufficient to prove this point, especially given that there are authentic narrations to support it, as follows:

Abū ᶜUmar reported on the authority of Abū ᶜUthmān al-Khūlānī that the Prophet (may God bless him and grant him peace) said, 'God (Blessed and Exalted is He) will continue to plant seeds in this religion and use them in His service.'[1] I say that He only plants these seeds because of the benefit they bring.

Suyūṭī quotes this *ḥadīth* in his *al-Jāmiᶜ al-ṣaghīr*, 'God will send to this community, at the start of every hundred years, someone to renew its religion for it.' Now I believe that this renewer (*mujaddid*) is not someone who follows the opinions of others, but rather takes directly from the Book of God and the *Sunna*[2] of His Messenger without any intermediaries; and he only makes use of what serves to renew the faith. The reader will not fail to observe the ambiguity of the language of the *ḥadīth*, and how this 'someone' could be one or many people.

In *al-Jāmiᶜ al-ṣaghīr*, he also relates the following *ḥadīth*, 'Every generation of my community will have its foremost.' And also, 'The earth is never without forty men like the Friend of the Compassionate (*Khalīl al-Raḥmān*).[3] By their means are you given rain, and by their means are you given aid. When one of them dies, God substitutes another in his stead.'

In sum, by researching the traditions on this matter one cannot fail to find something in the Muḥammadan community to please him. The Prophet (may God bless him and grant him peace) said, 'My community is like a garden tended by its owner. He weeds it, keeps its rows clear and straight, and prunes it, so that it becomes

1 We have chosen not to give the *ḥadīth* references as we feel that it is sufficient for the purpose of this translation that a scholar of the rank of the Shaykh al-ᶜAlawī has chosen and quoted them.

2 The *Sunna* means the doings or wont of the Prophet; his words, deeds and way of life. It constitutes the second source of authority in Islam after the Qur'ān.

3 Abraham.

more fruitful with each passing year. It may be that the last fruit it gives has the finest bunches and the longest stalks. By Him who sent me with the truth, the Son of Mary will surely find worthy replacements for his Disciples among my community.'[1] This is related in *al-Mabāḥith al-aṣliyya*.[2]

He also said, 'My community is a blessed community: no one knows if the first part or the last part is better.' And, 'My community is like rain: no one knows if the first part or the last part of it is more beneficial.'

Ṭabarānī narrates on the authority of Ibn ʿAbbās that the Messenger of God (may God bless him and grant him peace) said, 'Ah, if only I could meet my brothers!' They [the Companions] said, 'O Messenger of God, are we not your brothers?' He said, 'Nay. They are a people who will come after you. They will have faith like your faith, and believe in me as you believe in me, and help me as you help me. Ah, if only I could meet my brothers!'

Abū Jumuʿa al-Anṣārī said, 'I said, "O Messenger of God, will there ever be any people more greatly rewarded than us, since we believed in you and followed you?" He said, "And why would you not do so, when the Messenger of God is amongst you, bringing you revelation from Heaven? Nay, a people will come after you to whom the Book of God will come written on pages between covers, and they will believe in it and act on it; they shall be more greatly rewarded than you."' This was narrated by Aḥmad and Bukhārī in his *Tārīkh*, and quoted in *Fatḥ al-bayān*.

Now this does not mean that the latter generations are superior to, or even equal to, the very first and foremost such as the Emigrants;[3] I

1 The *ḥadīth* is referring to when Christ will return at the end of the present cycle of creation.

2 The Shaykh is presumably referring to *al-Futūḥāt al-ilāhiyya*, Ibn ʿAjība's commentary on Sarqusṭī's didactic Sufi poem *al-Mabāḥith al-aṣliyya*, (Damascus: al-Yamāma, 1986.), p. 86.

3 Those early Muslims who emigrated from Mecca to Medina before the conquest of Mecca.

would never say this. What I am saying is that just as only a deluded person would deny the virtue of the early generations, likewise only a wretched and intellectually bankrupt person would deny that this virtue still exists. Yet, often it is not that such ignorant people deny its existence, but that they deny ever having experienced it, since they are incapable of recognising it in anyone. What is good in the present is often veiled by dreams of the past. Or perhaps the reader might not deny that this virtue still endures, but doubts that we are worthy of it. In that case, this book of mine might be of use to those who come later, even if it does not please my contemporaries. *Say: I ask of you no payment for it, nor am I a pretender* [Q.XXXVIII.86]; *and you will come to know the truth about it in time* [Q.XXXVIII.88]; *and the best end will be for the reverent* [Q.VII.128].

Point Two: the Qur'ān has many facets and its wonders never cease, so the understanding of the ancients does not obviate the understanding of the latter generations.

The Book of God, the Almighty and All-Forgiving, has always delighted hearts, astounded minds and captivated thoughts. It is always a fresh meadow and an outspreading tree, to the extent that the one who interprets it would almost be adding to it were it not that *falsehood cannot approach it from any angle* [Q.XLI.42]. It is fresh and new in every age, and is the same now as it ever was. God said, and He continues to say, *Will they not meditate on this Qur'ān?* [Q.IV.82]. A tradition states that the Qur'ān's wonders never cease, which means that it must have many facets. Abū al-Dardā' (may God be pleased with him) is reported to have said, 'You will never have complete understanding until you see that the Qur'ān has many facets.' It is also said that this is a *ḥadīth* reported by Shaddād ibn Uways, as quoted by Ibn ʿAbd al-Barr.

This is also supported by the *ḥadīth*, 'The Qur'ān has an outward (*ẓāhir*), an inward (*bāṭin*), a boundary (*ḥadd*) and a horizon (*maṭlaʿ*)', as quoted in *Tāj al-tafāsīr*. Given this, do not be quick to disqualify what those with knowledge of God say about the Book of God. If it is beyond the reach of our minds, then we should deem it to be one of these four facets.

Moreover, do not suppose that these facets are found only in the Qur'ān as a whole; rather they are found in every single verse and every single word—we might even say in every single letter; after all, each letter is a Qur'ān just as the Book as a whole is a Qur'ān. This is why the Almighty says *We shall load you with speech of heavy weight* [Q.LXXIII.5] and *They who give ear to the speech and follow the best of it* [Q.XXXIX.18]. He uses the word 'speech' (*qawl*) rather than 'word' (*lafẓ*) or 'discourse' (*kalām*) in order to include both words and letters, since 'speech' encompasses them all. Every part of the Book of God—supposing that it can be divided into parts—is *of heavy weight* because of all the countless meanings it contains. Another proof that each letter of the Qur'ān is itself a Qur'ān is the *ḥadīth* narrated by Tirmidhī on the authority of Ibn Masʿūd stating that the Prophet said, 'Whoso recites a letter of the Book of God earns thereby a good deed, and every good deed is rewarded tenfold.' This makes clear that every individual letter is a Qur'ān in itself because of all the meanings it contains. Another narration has, 'I do not say that *alif-lām-mīm*[1] is a letter; rather *alif* is a letter, *lām* is a letter and *mīm* is a letter.'

This is why it is related that, 'Everything in the Book is in the *Fātiḥa*[2], and everything in the *Fātiḥa* is in *Bismi 'Llahi al-Raḥmān al-Raḥīm*.'[3] Another tradition adds, 'Everything in the *basmala* is in the letter *bā'*, and everything in the letter *bā'* is in the dot beneath it.' I wrote an epistle on this subject.[4]

1 A reference to the mysterious 'disjointed letters' (*muqaṭṭaʿāt*) that open certain Chapters of the Qur'ān.
2 The *Fātiḥa* is the first Chapter of the Qur'ān.
3 The formula *Bismi 'Llahi al-Raḥmān al-Raḥīm* ('In the Name of God, the Compassionate, the Merciful'), with which the Qur'ān opens and which appears before each but one of the Chapters of the Qur'ān. It is known as the *basmala* and a commentary on it follows this introduction.
4 *The Book of the Unique Archetype* (*al-Unmūdhaj al-farīd*). See Lings, *A Sufi Saint*, pp. 148-157.

Were it not for the marvels that the Book of God contains, we would not have been commanded to meditate on it through the ages. The Almighty says, *Will they not meditate on this Qur'ān?* [Q.IV.82]. The Prophet (may God bless him and grant him peace) said, 'Analyse the language of the Qur'ān, and seek out its marvels.' Now someone might say, 'God has relieved us of the burden of extracting its pearls by having those who came before us do it.' To this I reply: this would mean that we would lose out on our share of meditation on it—God forbid!—which no intelligent person would suggest, nor anyone graced with faith. If this were so, then the people of the second generation would not have spoken about it since the first generation had already done so, and the same thing for the third generation and so on. This shows that the Almighty Real did not single out any generation to meditate on it to the exclusion of others. Moreover, if only some had been singled out for this, it would mean that the meanings of the Qur'ān had been exhausted, when this is clearly not the case given that the Prophet (may God bless him and grant him peace) said that 'the Qur'ān's wonders never cease.' One of these wonders is that the one who meditates on it sees new marvels each day that he did not see the day before.

ʿAbd al-Wāḥid ibn Sulaymān reported that Ibn ʿAwn[1] used to say, 'There are three things I love for me and for my brethren…' one of them being 'that a man can meditate on this Qur'ān and contemplate it to the point where he stumbles upon knowledge he did not previously have.' This is also evidenced by the narration of Abū Nuʿaym and others stating that ʿAbd al-Raḥmān ibn Zayyān said, 'It was said to Moses (peace be upon him), "The scripture of Aḥmad[2] is like a pail of milk that continues to produce butter every time it is churned."'

All this is summarised in the words of Abū Bakr ibn al-ʿArabī[3] in *Funūn al-ta'wīl*, 'The total number of disciplines of the Qur'ān is

1 An early Muslim.
2 Meaning the Prophet Muḥammad.
3 The Mālikī jurist of Andalusia (d. 1148).

seventy-seven thousand four hundred and fifty[1] multiplied by four, since every word has an outward meaning, an inward meaning, a boundary and a horizon. Now this only refers to each individual word, and not to compounds and linking words, which are beyond reckoning and known only to God.'

The disciplines and facets of the Qur'ān can only be discovered by one who is spiritually realised.[2] As for those who are veiled, they are only *called from a distant place* [Q.XLI.44], listening from behind an iron curtain. They are barely in a position to properly grasp the outward meaning, never mind the inner meanings, and still less the boundary and the horizon. When God allows one to reach something of this, it would not be out of place for him to say as Imām ʿAlī (may God ennoble his countenance) said, 'If I desired, I could write enough commentary on the *Fātiḥa* to load the backs of forty camels.' (Or he said something of the sort.) Now you may say, 'But does the like of Imām ʿAlī exist today, with such knowledge as he had?' To this I reply: what a marvel, by God! Despite his great knowledge, only a few of the people of his time gave him his due, to the extent that he said from the pulpit, 'I am God's regent, whom you have overlooked.' Those who overlook the people of their own time now are akin to those who overlooked him then.

Point Three: there are disciplines in the Qur'ān that are not for popular consumption.

It may be that the one who cleaves to external things cannot see anything in the Book of God save that to which his own limited resources lead him, and so he denies everything else. He does not see that what he knows of the outward meaning of the Book is nothing more than the husk around the kernel, behind which lies 'what no eye has seen, nor ear heard, nor human heart imagined.'[3] Does he believe that his own understanding has lead him to what dwelt in

1 The number of words in the Qur'ān.
2 *Maftūḥ ʿalayh*, literally 'one who has received an opening'.
3 Reference to a well-known *ḥadīth* describing Paradise.

the inner cores of the Companions of the Prophet (may God bless him and grant him peace)? Of course not. Let him examine his soul, and see if his heart conceals something more precious than what his words contain. If it does, then he will be *one whom his Lord has made certain* [Q.XI.17]; and if not, then what he has lost is greater than what he has gained.

The Prophet (may God bless him and grant him peace) said, 'Some knowledge is, as it were, hidden, known only to those who have knowledge of God. When they reveal it, those who are ignorant of God deny it.' He also said, 'The knowledge of the inward is one of God's mysteries. God casts it into the heart of whomever of His servants He will.' He also said, 'Knowledge is of two kinds: knowledge in the heart, which is true beneficial knowledge; and knowledge on the tongue, which is God's proof against the Son of Adam.' This shows that there are hidden disciplines as well as disciplines for popular consumption. Abū Hurayra (may God be pleased with him) is well-known to have said, 'I have treasured in my memory two stores of knowledge from the Messenger of God (may God bless him and grant him peace). One I have divulged, but were I to divulge the other you would cut my throat.' This was related by Abū ʿUmar.

Ibn ʿAbbās (may God be pleased with him) is reported to have said, 'Were I to tell you what I know of the exegesis of God's words *The command descends between them* [Q.LXV.12], you would stone me to death, or call me an unbeliever.' Shaʿrānī[1] quoted this in *al-Yawāqīt wa'l-jawāhir*.

The following lines of poetry are attributed to Zayn al-ʿĀbidīn (may God be pleased with him),

> O Lord, were I to divulge a certain jewel of knowledge
> They would call me a worshipper of idols;
> And Muslim men would bay for my blood,
> And deem this vilest deed of theirs righteous!

1 The Egyptian jurist and Sufi (d. 1565).

Salmān al-Fārisī (may God be pleased with him) said, 'Were I to tell you all that I know, you would say, "May God have mercy on the one who kills Salmān."'

Imām ʿAlī (may God ennoble his countenance) said, 'There is certain knowledge in my possession—if I were to divulge it, you would separate this from this,' gesturing from his head to his body. The counsel he gave our master Kumayl ibn Ziyād[1] alludes to much of this; we shall give it here in full, despite its length, because of the indispensable wisdom it contains. He said, may God ennoble his countenance,

> O Kumayl, hearts are vessels, and the best of them are those which have the largest capacity for goodness. People are of three kinds: the divine sage (*ʿālim rabbānī*), one seeking knowledge for the sake of salvation, and riff-raff who go buzzing like flies around everything that attracts their attention; they do not seek the light of knowledge, nor look for refuge with a trusty support.
>
> There is knowledge here (he pointed at his heart)—would that I had found someone to bear it! I found one who had a sharp mind, but he could not be trusted with it, for he uses the religion as a tool for worldly gain: he uses God's proofs as arguments against His own Book, and His blessings as excuses to sin. Woe unto one who has the truth in his hands, but does not have the insight to see it! Doubt is cast into his heart by the least of suspicions, so that he does not know where the truth is. When he speaks he errs, and knows not of his error. He is distracted by things, but does not know what they really are. He is a test to those who are charmed by with him.
>
> All good is in the one to whom God teaches his religion; and lack of knowledge of his religion is sufficient ignorance. See, then, how knowledge dies with the death of those who bear it. Yet the earth will

1 A companion of Imām ʿAlī.

> never be bereft of those who uphold God's proofs, whether they be known publically or hidden, so that His proofs and messages are not erased. Yet how rare they are! By God, they are the fewest in number but the greatest in stature. By them does He defend His proofs and messages, that they may convey them to their contemporaries and plant them in the hearts of their peers. Knowledge raised them up to the level of true insight, connecting them to the spirit of certitude. They find easy what worldly people find impossible, and they are content with what ignorant people cannot abide. They live in this world in their bodies, but their spirits are attached to the Supreme Realm. They are God's vicegerents on His earth, and the teachers of His religion. Ah, ah, how I long to see them!

The essence of all that we have related here is that all the teachings of the books of old amount to only a fraction of what is contained in hearts, *And that which is with God is better for the virtuous* [Q.III.198].

Point Four: the Qur'ān is addressed to us all equally, and not only to certain people in certain times.

The Qur'ān is the Word of God through which He speaks to His servants, though they perceive it not, and a scripture He sent directly to them, though they know it not. *Distracted are their hearts* [Q.XXI.3]. It is as though they think it is all over and done with, and now they merely take their rulings from it without actually being the ones to whom it was addressed. They act as though they are saying, 'It was only revealed to Muḥammad and the people with him,' and they take it merely by way of following, not by direct and independent contact with it. Heaven preserve us! The Prophet (may God bless him and grant him peace) said, 'I am the messenger of those I meet alive, and those born after me.' When it comes to the address itself, all those to whom the message was sent are equal. When God says, *O you who believe*, He is speaking to every believer. Do not say that He 'said'; rather He *says* it, right now, whether we are aware of it or not. When

God opens one's insight, one sees it as being *brought down by the Trusted Spirit* [Q.XXVI.193] right now; and when one reads it, one reads it from *a manifest book* [Q.XXXVI.12]. The greatest in rank are those who receive it directly from the Most Merciful, few though they be. Do not find this far-fetched, since after all it is the Word of God and no one else's. Indeed, everyone believes it is the Word of God, yet they fail to hear it from God; no one can hear it from God unless God is his hearing, 'When I love him, I am his hearing...'[1] Attributes cannot be separated from what they describe.[2] Yet it only emerges from behind a veil which covers it: *It is not for any man that God should speak to him, save by revelation or from behind a veil* [Q.LXI.51].

When Moses (peace be upon him) heard the voice from the right side of Mt Sinai, he recognised it as God's voice without needing any further proof, because of the sound sensitivity and taste he had been granted. Likewise, when one of us grows stronger in certitude and his inner being expands with the words of the Qur'ān he hears, he deems them nothing other than words God is speaking to him in that very instant, and needs no further proof of this because of the profound impact it has on his heart.

Ṭabarānī narrated on the authority of al-Nawwās ibn Samʿān that the Prophet said, 'When God speaks revelation, Heaven begins to tremble violently in fear of God, and when the denizens of Heaven hear this they swoon and fall down prostrate. The first one who raises his head is Gabriel (peace be upon him), and God conveys unto him what He wants to reveal. He then takes this to all the other angels; each time he passes through a heaven its denizens ask him, "What does our Lord say?", and he replies, "The Truth." Then he takes it where he is commanded.'

Likewise, when Gabriel took it down to Muḥammad (may God bless him and grant him peace), the power of the revelation would cause him [the Prophet] to shake in his bones; and it continues to

1 Sacred *ḥadīth*.
2 That is, God and His attributes are one.

have this power. Whenever it visits an unsullied heart, it has a powerful impact on it. Praise be to God, a share in this was allotted to me, so that whenever I heard the Word of God I would tremble in awe of it and feel as though I could hear the echo of a bell; and when I picked up the Qur'ān, I held it as reverently as if it were a message delivered to me personally from the All-Wise and All-Knowing, beginning (after the *Fātiḥā*): *In the Name of God, the Compassionate, the Merciful. Alif-lām-mīm. This beyond doubt is the Book* [Q.II.1-2]. Then I would take it and read it as eagerly as a lonely man reads a letter from his family, delighting in it and not feeling satisfied until he has read everything in it. By means of this favour—God be praised—God allowed me to glimpse some of its jewels. Now do not think that what I have written here is the sum of all that I have understood, or even a tenth of it; for 'The wonders of the Qur'ān never cease.'

AN IMPORTANT NOTE: The Holy Qur'ān was revealed to the Companions of Muḥammad in stages. This is true of how it was revealed to them; but when it comes to how it was revealed to *us*, it came to us from God as a whole, through the intermediary of those by whom God preserved it until our time. It was God who preserved it, *We Ourselves sent down the Remembrance, and We preserve it* [Q.XV.9]. This applies to those who came before us, and will apply to those who come after us.

Our words 'it came to us from God as a whole' are supported by the aforementioned *ḥadīth* of Abū Jumuʿa al-Anṣārī, 'I said, "O Messenger of God, will there ever be any people more greatly rewarded than us, since we believed in you and followed you?" He said, "And why would you not do so, when the Messenger of God is amongst you, bringing you revelation from Heaven? Nay, a people will come after you to whom the Book of God will come written on pages between covers, and they will believe..."' The key words here are 'to whom the Book of God will come written on pages between covers', which tells us beyond doubt that the Book of God is addressed to us directly, and we are not simply reading what was addressed to someone else before us.

When we say that the Qur'ān came to us as a whole, we are referring to its words. Its meanings, however, are still in the care of the Trusted Spirit, who brings them down to the hearts of those of the community of Muḥammad (may God bless him and grant him peace) who are completely ready to receive them. He brings them in stages, as they are needed, just as once the words of the Qur'ān themselves were brought down in stages. Do not find it far-fetched that meanings could be brought down to the hearts of the gnostics by angels: *Those who say, 'Our Lord is God' and then follow straight His path, on them descend the angels* [Q.XLI.30]. If this is still not clear to you, consider the *ḥadīth*, 'The earth is never without forty men like the Friend of the Compassionate'—how close the angels are to hearts like the heart of God's Friend! The hearts of the gnostics are occupied by the Supreme Assembly,[1] and this is why they partake in the mystical knowledge of the angels. Aḥmad ibn Abī al-Ḥawārī said to Imam Aḥmad ibn Ḥanbal (may God be pleased with them both), 'I heard my shaykh, Ibn Samʿān, say, "When souls become used to abstaining from sin, they rise up into the angelic realm and then bring back rare pieces of wisdom to their owners, without any human teacher conveying it to them." Aḥmad ibn Ḥanbal said, "You speak the truth, Aḥmad, and so did your shaykh."'

I say, then, that God Almighty continues to explain the meanings of the Qur'ān in every age and time. He said, and He continues to say, *When We recite it, follow its recitation; and then it is upon Us to explain it* [Q.LXXV.18–19]. One aspect of the explanation He has undertaken to give is found in the meanings God causes to come forth on the tongues of His chosen elect. In His wisdom, He only reveals to the sages (*ʿulamā'*) of each age what the people of that age require; by 'sages' here, we mean those who truly implement the knowledge they inherit and uphold God's proof to the world—those by means of whom God preserves this religion until they pass it on to those who come after them. We do not mean those prattlers *whose efforts*

1 *Al-Mala' al-Aʿlā*, meaning the angels.

have been wasted in this life [Q.XVIII.104]; they are visited by none but the hosts of Satan, who give them the means with which they would unravel the religion, were it not that *God abolishes that which Satan casts and then establishes His revelations* [Q.XXII.52].

Point Five: every word of the Qur'ān concerns everyone in every time.
Once we reflect on how the Qur'ān is a book from God Almighty addressed directly to us, we cannot consider any of God's warnings or promises therein to refer to other people. Rather, if any one of them is applicable to someone, this means it is indeed addressed to him personally. The same applies to all the commandments, prohibitions, encouragements and discouragements. This is one way in which the Book is addressed to us.

As for the historical circumstances of the revelation of certain verses, which seem to suggest that they were intended for specific people, this only means that the people in question served as the means by which the description or ruling was issued for a particular person-type. We should reflect on the broad meaning of God's words, not the narrow circumstances of their revelation. 'Souls are hosts arrayed',[1] all equally able to relate to what is addressed to them; they do not precede one another in time in the way that bodies do. For example, the souls of all hypocrites, from the time of the very first of them[2] to the last of them, are all addressed by the Qur'ānic warnings to hypocrites, and those verses were revealed about every single one of their kind. The same applies to all the other types of people the Qur'ān addresses. To deny this would be to make a dead letter out of a great deal of the Qur'ānic text. I do not believe that there is a single dead letter in the Book of God; everything in it can be applied to those who fit the bill in every age, or in every moment even. This means that all its words pass from one addressee to the

1 *Ḥadīth*.
2 Meaning the *munāfiqūn* of Medina who pretended to profess Islam but were actually working against it.

next at all times, falling in their proper places without any addition or subtraction.

More wondrous still is that even the words addressed literally to the Prophet (may God bless him and grant him peace) could also apply figuratively to his spiritual heirs, by way of allusion. Conversely, anything therein that seemed to warn him or ascribe a shortcoming to him can be applied literally to his heirs, since they are more likely than him to be actually guilty of shortcomings. When the Muḥammadan *quṭb*,[1] or one who has a heart like the heart of our liege Abraham (upon them both be blessings and peace), hears God's words *O Prophet* or *O Messenger, convey that which has been sent down to you* [Q.v.67], he sees this as nothing other than a command from God to him personally telling him to convey the teachings of the religion. This is the wisdom (and God knows best) behind His not addressing him [the Prophet] in His Glorious Book by his name by saying 'O Muḥammad' or 'O Aḥmad' as he addresses all the other prophets (may God bless them and grant them peace), but rather calling him *O Prophet* [Q.xxxiii.1]; *O Messenger* [Q.v.41]; *O you who are wrapped in your garment* [Q.lxxiii.1]; *O you who are wrapped in your cloak* [Q.lxxiv.1] and so on. This allows the addresses to apply to his spiritual heirs who convey his teachings as well, by way of allusion: 'The sages are the heirs of the prophets,'[2] and those who convey the teachings of the messengers are their heirs. Do you not see that when Jesus (peace be upon him) sent his Apostles to Antioch, God called them 'messengers' and declared that He Himself had sent them, saying *We sent them two, but they denied them, so We strengthened them with a third* [Q.xxxvi.14]. So there is nothing to prevent anyone from the Muḥammadan community who delivers his teachings being called by the Qur'ān in this way, and being the one intended by it in God's knowledge. Do you not see that He also called Muḥammad in

1 The *quṭb* in Sufi terminology is the Pole, the living head of the hierarchy of saints around whom the others 'turn'.
2 *Ḥadīth*.

the Torah and elsewhere in the same way, saying 'Gird your sword upon your thigh, O most mighty!' [Psalms 45:3]?[1] This address too could have applied metaphorically to someone else in that age, the literal meaning being saved for the Prophet (may God bless him and grant him peace).

As for the wisdom behind God calling the other prophets by their names alone, it is (and God knows best) that their Laws were not destined to last forever, unlike the Law (*sharīʿa*) of our Prophet. It will last forever and calling [others] by means of it[2] applies to every prophetic spiritual heir until finally passing on to the Mahdī and then to Jesus (peace be upon them both). When God commands Muḥammad (may God bless him and grant him peace), he commands them both; when He addresses him, He addresses them. This is why He addresses him [in the Qur'ān] with *O you who*.

Know also that the true conveyor of the teachings of the Qur'ān past, present and future is none other than Muḥammad (may God bless him and grant him peace). His light, hidden within his vicegerents (*khulafā'*), is what hears the calls addressed to him. He (may God bless him and grant him peace) said, 'God have mercy on my vicegerents! God have mercy on my vicegerents!' They said, 'Who are your vicegerents, Messenger of God?' He said, 'They who love my *Sunna*, and teach it to God's servants.' This was narrated by Ibn ʿAbd al-Barr.

What makes us even more aware of this point is that the word *Say* has not been removed from the recitation or written text of the Qur'ān, even though it is not a necessary part of the content of what is said. When God said to His Prophet *Say: 'I have no control over benefit or harm for myself, save as God wills'* [Q.VII.188], the mind immediately registers *I have no control over benefit or harm for myself* without the word, *Say*. The reason this word is retained it that is a permanently active verb like any other, and applies to everyone who ought to say

1 This passage from the Psalms is often interpreted by Muslims as referring to the Prophet.
2 That is, by means of the Muḥammadan *sharīʿa*.

these words whenever he understands that God wills this. We are speaking here about the spiritual Muḥammadan heir. If the word *Say* were removed, our share would be diminished; or we might say that our understanding of the Book of God would be diminished. None understand this save those endowed with sagacity.

Point Six: the most important thing to remember about the Qur'ān is that one should see it as coming directly to one from the Presence of the Compassionate. The most important thing for us to bear in mind when approaching the Qur'ān is that we should see it as coming directly to us from God's Presence right now, in the form in which it has between its covers, declaring of itself, *This beyond doubt is the Book* [Q.II.2]. That this is indeed the way in which it comes to us from God is affirmed by the aforementioned *ḥadīth* of Abū Jumuʿa.

It is clear that God's Book comes from no one but God. The fact that the Book was compiled and arranged in its present form and then sent out to the world by the Companions (may God be pleased with them) should not cause you any difficulty. Indeed it was them who did this, but they did it as God's channels. He says, *We Ourselves sent down the Remembrance, and We preserve it* [Q.XV.9]. God undertook to preserve it just as He had undertaken to send it down, and therefore in reality it was He who compiled it and arranged it according to the form already ordained for it in His knowledge. This refers to the arrangement of the Chapters (*Sūra*, pl. *Suwar*), since there is a dispute as to whether this was taken directly from the Prophet or was done by the reasoning of the Companions. As for the arrangement of the verses (*āya*, pl. *āyāt*) within the Chapters, there is consensus that this was done according to revelation from God, as the traditions make clear. Jalāl al-Dīn Suyūṭī quotes Qāḍī Abū Bakr [ibn al-ʿArabī] as saying, 'Our view is that all the Qur'ān that God sent down and ordered to be kept and written, and did not abrogate, is what is present between the covers of the written copy of ʿUthmān, with no omissions or additions. It is arranged and ordered as ordained by God

Himself and directed by His Messenger.' It came down surrounded by light and angels, and its meanings were transmitted by inspiration (*waḥy*) from God to those hearts ready to receive it.

Aḥmad narrates in his *Musnad* on the authority of Maʿqal ibn Yassār that the Messenger of God (may God bless him and grant him peace) said, '*Al-Baqara* is the peak and summit of the Qur'ān; with every verse of it descended eighty angels.' Do you suppose that those angels who came down to earth with this Chapter delivered it and then just left it on earth alone? Of course not. By God's aid, His Book will continue to be surrounded by angels until God calls the earth and all upon it back to Himself; *All things return to God* [Q.XLII.53]. Do not worry if some demonic people interfere with individual copies of it, for it is preserved and spread through the world in its proper state.

As for *Sūrat al-Baqara* being the peak and summit of it, this shows that God Himself arranged it in His eternal knowledge, and that the Messenger of God (may God bless him and grant him peace) knew of its final form.

Commentary on the *Basmala* from *The Swelling Sea: An Exegesis of the Qur'ān by Pure Light*

Bism 'Llāh al-Raḥmān al-Raḥīm

In the Name of God, the Compassionate, the Merciful

That the Mighty Book begins, when read and when written, with the *basmala* inspires in us a sense of God's kindness to His creatures, despite how they turn away from Him. For whenever one reads or recites the book, moving one's eye over the page or moving one's tongue in the recitation, one is connected to *In the Name of God, the Compassionate, the Merciful*, and thus one invokes the Name (*al-Ism*)[1] and draws blessing from it without even being aware of this, whether one intends it or not, whether one likes it or not. Had we not been commanded to write it down, intentions would have varied, and heedlessness would have come to bear, and even those of strong faith would have forgotten it; and hypocrites would have affected to forget it. Yet since the *basmala* is prescribed for both the writing and recitation of the Qur'ān, this possibility has been nullified.

As for the prescription that the *basmala* be invoked before every action of importance, its effect is to nullify any special distinction that would be otherwise afforded to tyrants, so that no overwhelming power is attributed to one person over another. Non-Islamic communities, both of the ancients and the moderns, used to seek blessing by invoking the names of their kings and rulers; for example, one of them might invoke the name of the king or ruler before drinking,

1 Meaning here *Allāh*.

especially if he were in his presence. Now since Islam preaches human equality and affirms that superiority over others can only be attained by mindfulness of reverence to God,[1] the Lawgiver commanded that no name be invoked before significant actions but the Name of God. The only exception being such actions as the Law forbids; for the Name of God could not possibly be a support for them. The wisdom of this is that since the Almighty has not permitted the action, He is saying, as it were, 'I have not made this lawful for you, nor given you leave to do it, which means that you have made it lawful for yourself; do it, then, in your own name, not in Mine.' A law is attributed to the one who makes it.

Now the letter *bā'* of the *basmala* [meaning 'in'] implies connection, and it is itself connected [directly] to God (*'Llāh*); the word 'Name' (*Ism*) does not separate them, since it is identical with the Named according to the Sufis as well as most of the Ashʿarīs.[2] Thus the beginning is in God (*bi'Llāh*): from Him all begins and to Him all returns.

JURIDICAL:[3] Four rulings can be deduced from the *basmala*: Firstly, all who write or recite the Qur'ān must begin with the *basmala*; this is inferred from that fact that the Almighty Himself begins the Book with it.

Secondly, we understand from this that God wishes us to praise Him for His Beauty more so that His Majesty; this is inferred from how He begins with the two Holy Names 'the Compassionate' (*al-Raḥmān*) and 'the Merciful' (*al-Raḥīm*), describing His Essence (*Dhāt*) thereby.

Thirdly, we learn that there is a difference between the two Names,

1 Allusion to verse Q.XLIX.13: *...the noblest of you, in the sight of God, is the one most mindful of Him.*

2 When the *basmala* is written in Arabic, the letter *bā'*, 'in', is directly connected to the word *ism*, 'Name'. What the Shaykh al-ʿAlawī is saying is that since the Name (*Ism*) is identical with the Named, i.e. God Himself, *Ism* does not really separate the letter *bā'* from the Divine Name *Allāh*.

3 Note that the Shaykh al-ʿAlawī does not list the four levels on interpretation in a fixed order, or even refer to all four levels for every passage he discusses, instead preferring to give them as and when they occur to him.

though they are derived from a single Quality;[1] for otherwise, to list both 'the Compassionate' and 'the Merciful' would be nothing but repetition.

Fourthly, we learn that the Name is identical with the Named; otherwise, it would not be proper to seek aid in it rather than its object, God (*Allāh*).

ALLEGORICAL: The way the letter *bā'* is fastened to the Divine Name,[2] though it is not part of it, inspires in us a consciousness of how everything in existence, with all its different realities and divergent paths, is fastened to God. Do not imagine that it touches Him—for in His transcendence, our Lord is not touched by any contingent thing, and such could not occur without the contingent thing vanishing altogether because of its lack of permanence in the presence of Him who is Eternal—rather, we mean that it is connected to Him and given being through Him: it subsists through God; not through itself. Its being is borrowed from that of its Being-Giver (*mūjid*), as it has been said:

> That which has no being in and of itself
> Could not be at all, were it not that He is.

The way the *bā'* of the *basmala* is lengthened where otherwise it is not,[3] is because it is connected to the Name, and the one who is connected to the Named—and is thus one of God's Folk—is worthy of being raised above the other members of his kind. As for the lengthened *bā'*'s standing in for the elided letter *alif* of the word *ism*, it symbolises the

1 They are both derived from *raḥma*.
2 We have chosen to translate *Ism al-Jalāla*, the 'Name of Majesty', as the Divine Name because the expression is used in Arabic to refer to the Divine Name *Allāh*.
3 In the *basmala*, the first downward stroke of the letter *bā'* is often lengthened, particularly in North African orthography, so that it is as tall as a letter *alif*, because it serves the function of representing both the letter *bā'* and the *alif* of the word *ism*, 'Name.' See Martin Lings, *A Sufi Saint*, p. 156.

representation[1] of God by he who possesses the Muḥammadan inheritance: *O David, We have made you a vicegerent on earth* [Q.XXXVIII.26]; *Whoso obeys the Messenger has obeyed God* [Q.IV.80].

As for the position of the *basmala* at the head and summit of the Book, it symbolises how God is raised above His Throne; and since this 'rising' (*istiwā'*)[2] does not mean, as ordinary people think, that He is 'contained' by the Throne, but rather that He is present in every element of existence, the *basmala* is placed at the head of every Chapter of the Qur'ān (*Sūra*),[3] whether short or long: *And He is with you, wherever you are* [Q.LVII.4].

Traditions affirm that everything in the Book is encapsulated in the words 'In the Name of God, the Compassionate, the Merciful'; this symbolises how all things are contained in the Being of their Being-Giver; that is, that everything in them branches from what is in Him: *Nor is there anything but with Us are the treasuries thereof* [Q.XV.21]. That the Divine Name [*Allāh*] comes before the other Beautiful Names[4] symbolises the precedence of the Essence, and how the Names and Qualities are contained in Its treasury. The first of the Names to be proclaimed thereafter is *The Compassionate* (*al-Raḥmān*)*: ask any informed of Him!* [Q.XXV.59]; because of this, it among all Names is given in the *basmala* to describe Him. Were it not that it was the first Name to be manifested, it would not have been assigned the position of 'rising' (*istiwā'*): *The Compassionate, raised upon the Throne* [Q.XX.5]. Because of this 'rising', this Name has precedence over all other Names, both

1 We have translated the word *niyāba* as both 'standing in' and 'representation'. The Shaykh is saying that the letter *bā'* is lengthened to represent the *alif* in the same way that a prophet or saint is God's intermediary and His representative.
2 Allusion to Qur'ānic verses such as: X.3 and XIII.2.
3 In fact it is placed at the head of all Chapters but one, the exception being *Sūrat al-Tawba* (Chapter IX).
4 The Beautiful Names (*al-Asmā' al-Ḥusnā*) are the Names of God, referred to as such in the verse: *God's are the most Beautiful Names, so call on Him by them* (Q.VII.180) and traditionally said to number ninety-nine based on a famous *ḥadīth*, although the exact identity of the ninety-nine is not agreed upon and several lists exist. See Lings, *The Holy Qur'ān*, pp. 205-211 for a translation of the most common list.

those of Majesty and those of Beauty. This is alluded to in those sacred *ḥadīth*[1] which affirm that mercy has precedence over wrath. The rising of the Compassionate over all beings is what allows the unbeliever to receive divine favours, and what allowed Satan to rebel.

As for His Name 'the Merciful' (*al-Raḥīm*), it is the last of the revelations,[2] and its effect is hidden within the actions of created beings. This is alluded to in the *ḥadīth*s, 'The merciful are shown mercy by God,' and, 'To fail to thank people is to fail to thank God.' The presence of His mercy in them means that they merit thanks; and all thanks is due to God.

Now the *bā'* of the *basmala* requires a verb to give it context,[3] and this verb is here elided. This symbolises how a Quality (*ṣifa*) requires a context to make its manifestation necessary; and this context is provided by the Act of the Essence, but it is elided; which is to say that it is only supposed (*muqaddar*), but has no being of its own independent from its Being-Giver. This is the difference between the two kinds of being. As to whether it comes before or after the Quality, this depends on the perspective of the given spiritual wayfarer. He who is immersed in the divine Magnificence will not see it at all, nor will he describe it either with being or nonbeing, never mind see it as coming before or after. As for he who has attained the level of sensitivity (*shuʿūr*), he will suppose it to come after, because he sees the Almighty before he sees His Act, and sees in God evidence of it. As for the ordinary wayfarer, he will see the Act before he sees He who acts, and the former will guide him to the latter. What a difference there is between one who sees Him as evidence, and one who sees other things as evidence for Him!

SPIRITUAL: The short vowel *kasra* on the letter *bā'* resembles the first person genitive pronoun as it is pronounced in certain dialects.[4] In

1 *Ḥadīth* are the sayings of the Prophet; the 'sacred *ḥadīth*' (*ḥadīth qudsī*) are sayings of the Prophet where God speaks on the tongue of the Prophet.

2 In the sense that it is the last word of the *basmala*, which here symbolises the whole of the Qur'ān.

3 That is, it requires us to say 'I begin in the Name of God', or the like.

4 That is, the first syllable *bi* in *bismi'Llāh* resembles the compound *bī*, meaning 'in me' or 'through me'.

this is hidden a secret expression: 'Through me (*bī*) is all that is, and through me is all that will be.' This [me] indicates the active quality the Sufis call 'the handful of light.'[1] It says—by means of the *bā'* attached to the Supreme Name—to the Eternal Presence and the Hidden Treasure, 'Through me (*bī*) is the Name of God; You have manifested me just as I manifested You; just as You raised me, I raised You; just as You made me known, I made You known.' Speaking from its state, it says,

> If not for You, we would not be; and if not for us, You would not be;[2]
> You are, and we are, and the truth cannot be known.
> To You we ascribe all glory and wealth;
> To us we ascribe poverty, yet poverty there is none.

So the All-Powerful has power through the objects of His power, and the All-Seeing has sight through the objects of His sight, and so on.

Now since the Acts manifest the Names and Qualities but not the Essence, the *bā'* is connected to the Name (*bism*) and not directly to the Named (*Allāh*), which ensures that we understand it is the Name that it manifests. As for the Essence, It is the reason for this pronoun on the *bā'* being concealed. For He is Outwardly Manifest in His Essence as long as His Act is not taken into consideration; when the Act *is* taken into consideration, however, we say that He is Inwardly Hidden in His Essence and Outwardly Manifest in His Qualities.

1 Referring to a Sufi tradition, sometimes thought to be a *ḥadīth*, which states that creation began with a handful of God's own Light.

2 The Shaykh is saying that the *bā'* represents the intermediary between God and creation, and that without this intermediary God would not be known, and thus 'would not be' in a metaphorical sense since His existence would be a secret. In the language of Ibn ʿArabī, this is expressed by the *ilāh/ma'lūh* relationship: in order that He be *ilāh* ('divine') in the full sense of the word, a *ma'lūh* or 'divine thrall' is required to recognise Him. See William Chittick, *The Sufi Path of Knowledge*, p. 60.

Commentary on the 'Opening of the Book' (*al-Fātiḥa*) from *The Swelling Sea: An Exegesis of the Qur'ān by Pure Light*

In the Name of God, the Compassionate, the Merciful
Praise be to God, Lord of the worlds
The Compassionate, the Merciful
King of the Day of Judgement
You we worship, and from You we seek help
Guide us upon the straight path
The path of those upon whom is Your grace, not of those upon whom is wrath, nor those who are astray

Concerning the question of whether the *basmala* is a verse of the *Fātiḥa*, or a verse of every *Sūra*, or not a verse in any *Sūra* save for *Sūrat al-Naml*,[1] there are different interpretations and it is better not to make a definitive pronouncement on the matter, and to recite it at the start of every *Fātiḥa* in the prayer to be on the safe side.

The meaning of *Fātiḥat al-Kitāb* is '*the* Opening of the Book' and not '*an* opening of the Book'; in reality the Book is 'of' the *Fātiḥa*, because it [the *Fātiḥa*] contains all its teachings. Yet if we say that it

1 The words *In the Name of God, the Compassionate, the Merciful* occur midway through *Sūrat al-Naml* (Q.XXVII.30), quoting the letter from Solomon to the Queen of Sheba. Since the formula is in the middle of the Chapter and part of its narrative rather than a prefix at the beginning, there is no dispute as to its being part of the Qur'ān. Whether the *basmala* formulas prefixing every Chapter of the Qur'ān except the *Sūrat al-Tawba* are actual verses of those Chapters, or additions to them meant to introduce them, is a subject of debate among Muslim scholars.

is an 'opening' or 'mother' (*umm*)[1] for it, this means that it is separate from it just as the mother is separate from her child; this explains why this name was not written in some of the manuscripts of the Companions.[2] It is beyond the reach of the average intellect to understand how it can be both outside it and inside it.

ALLEGORICAL: The Essence of the Maker (*Dhāt al-Bārī*) is both distinct from the cosmos and present in it: distinct with respect to transcendence (*tanzīh*) and present with respect to immanence (*qayyūmiyya*). Neither of these must be viewed in isolation, because to affirm only the former would be to suggest separation, and to affirm only the latter would be to suggest connection; both are impossible, because in reality there is nothing to be separated from Him or connected to Him. Do not be deluded by the appearance of shadows, for to imagine something does not give it independent existence. Things are only multiplied or added to like by like, and there is nothing like the Real.

The wisdom in the *Fātiḥa*'s position at the beginning of the Book is that it speaks of mercy from God for the reader, and offers a teaching and instruction on the proper way to offer the gratitude one owes, making one fit to have a connection to Him, which is a favour for which no thanks could be enough. The individual human being could never have deduced this for himself, no matter how long he reflected on the matter, for he could never determine what the proper expression of praise should be, or the proper way to recite the Book and stand before God seeking nearness to Him. Thus the *Fātiḥa* came from God to provide us with all this, and God makes it pass through the lips of all those who recite the Book; whether they intend it or not, they offer a measure of gratitude, for the first thing God causes to pass their lips is the dedication of all forms of praise to Him [*al-ḥamdu li'Llāh*], and then an acknowledgement of His Lordship which is

1 The *Fātiḥa* is traditionally known as '*umm al-kitāb*' (mother of the Book) but the Shaykh al-ʿAlawī contests this here.

2 That is, included as a title for the Chapter when the oral Qur'ān was written down by the Companions.

exclusively His in all the worlds [*Rabb al-ʿālamīn*], as the wording entails. And since the subject of a lord might acknowledge his lordship without having any inclination towards or affection for him, He then draws them nigh and inspires their affection by telling them that this Lord whose subjects they are is the Compassionate (*al-Raḥmān*), the Merciful (*al-Raḥīm*), so that the servant-lord relationship will be one of desire, not fear. Then, after they become sure of His grace and are happily settled between these two Names, He fears lest they be so immersed in His mercies that they forget their duties of worship, and so He moves them on to the station of justice, first attracting them with Beauty and then warning them with Majesty, so that they are given further strength and stability by His words *King of the Day of Judgement* [*Māliki yawm al-dīn*]. And since He causes them to speak of the Quality of Justice, and the inevitability of the Day of Judgement, their natures demand that they then be allowed recourse to an impenetrable fortress; thus He taught them to say, *You we worship, and from You we seek help* [*Iyyāka naʿbudu wa-Iyyāka nastaʿīn*]. The first half of the verse establishes justice, and the second effects grace; and since the first half cannot exist on its own because it usually requires supports, and the second half is extremely difficult to attain and is usually a matter of a prayer of the tongue which requires focus, He taught them how to ask for guidance to that straight way by saying, *Guide us upon the straight path* [*ihdinā al-ṣirāṭ al-mustqīm*]. Now since the individual might forge for himself his own path, the Almighty qualified this by saying, *The path of those upon whom is Your grace, not of those upon whom is wrath, nor those who are astray* [*ṣirāṭ al-ladhīna anʿamta ʿalayhim ghayri al-maghḍūbi ʿalayhim wa-lā 'ḍ-ḍālīn*]. This makes it clear that the path sought in the *Sūra* is that of those who hold to the *Sunna* and the Community (*ahl al-sunna wa'l-jamāʿa*).

In His perfect kindness, God does not prefix the *Fātiḥā* with the word 'Say,' as He usually does when prompting speech from us, as in *Say: God is One* [Q.CXII.1], or *Say: Praise be to God* [Q.XXVII.59] in other places in the Qur'ān. All this is so that the servant is truly the one offering the praise, saying 'Praise be to God' as he stands before Him in prayer or recites the Book; and this would not be the case were it to have begun with 'Say: Praise be to God.'

ALLEGORICAL: Part of worship is servitude, and the Laws of God contain secrets which are beyond the reach, not only of normal sight, but of inner sight as well; it is these secrets which make it possible for one to stand before God even if one is affecting a state which is not truly his, and deny it to another even if he is engaged in outward worship. Were it not that prayer has a goal, and that the way has a destination, God would not make the servant ask, as he prays, to be guided to the straight path.[1] We understand from this that the acts of the body are not the goal; since otherwise, this would be a request for something already obtained.

Praise be to God, Lord of the worlds [Q.I.2]

EXEGETICAL: Praise (*ḥamd*) means to acknowledge beauty and goodness as they deserve to be acknowledged. The definite article *al-* that is prefixed to *ḥamd* implies universality,[2] and the preposition 'to' (*li*) before 'God' (*'Llāhi*) implies rightful ownership; thus the meaning is that praise, as it is, and whichever tongue speaks it, all ultimately goes back to God, whether the speaker is aware of this or not. He is the Object of every tongue's praise, and every heart's worship; for, since all beauty is borrowed from His Beauty, all praise is praise of Him: *To God prostrate all who are in the heavens and the earth, willingly or unwillingly* (Q.XIII.15). Thus it is said, 'Whenever they praise, and whatever they praise, they praise naught but Him; and whenever they worship, and whatever they worship, they worship naught but Him.' Moreover, the Divine Name [*Allāh*] is the given name of the Essence, unto which all praises are due; and therefore all praise belongs to it alone among the Names, since no one Name of

1 That is, were prayer its own goal, it would not make sense to ask to be guided to the straight path while praying, since one would already be on it.

2 The Arabic literally says 'the praise' (*al-ḥamd*), meaning 'all praise', or 'praise' as a class.

a Quality deserves all manners of praises as the Name of the Essence deserves them.

As for the Name 'Lord' (*Rabb*), it is more fitting to be mentioned in connection to 'the worlds' than any other, which is why they are ascribed to it here. He undertakes to preserve and sustain the worlds however many there are, and however far they stretch; and the kindness of this Name [*Rabb*], and His sustenance of all that exists, is manifested in that He is concerned with His individual servant, almost to the point where it seems that He has no other servant but him; yet the servant is heedless of Him and disobedient to Him, almost to the point where it seems that he has several lords. Were he to reflect on how the Lord has sustained him from the point where he left his father's loins for his mother's womb, and then became a morsel of flesh, and then developed until finally he was a being possessed of hearing and sight, he would proclaim *Blessed be God, the Fairest of creators!* [Q.XXIII.14].

As for the 'worlds' (*ʿālamīn*), this is an expression for all things other than God. That it is given in the plural here implies that God possesses an infinite number of worlds. The Prophet (may God bless him and grant him peace) said, 'God Almighty has eighteen thousand worlds, all like this world of yours.' Abū Saʿīd al-Khudrī[1] narrated, 'God has forty thousand worlds; this lower world, from East to West, is one of them' (Shabrakhītī narrated this). Kaʿb al-Aḥbār[2] said, 'No one but God knows how many worlds there are.' This suggests that the numbers given in the aforementioned traditions are only meant to show how high the number is, rather than to state it definitively. Those who say that this planet Earth is the only world have no reason for saying so other than their lack of attentiveness to the vastness of God's dominion. Were any man to simply look around him, he would realise that he is ignorant of far more than he knows; and were he to observe closely any small planet, he would find there creatures

1 A Companion of the Prophet.
2 An early convert to Islam.

of God. Simply to reflect on the minuteness of a germ is enough to realise this. Ghazālī (may God be pleased with him) reported that the Messenger of God (may God bless him and grant him peace) went to see his Companions one day, and found them deep in thought. He asked them why they were not speaking, and they said, 'We are meditating upon the creation of God Almighty.' He answered, 'Indeed, that is what you should do: meditate upon His creation, but do not meditate upon Him; for beyond this sunset is a white land, whose light is its whiteness and its whiteness is its light. The sun passes over it in the course of forty [of our] days, and upon it are creatures of God Almighty who have never disobeyed Him, even for the blinking of an eye.' 'O Messenger of God,' they said, 'does Satan not afflict them?' He answered, 'They know not that Satan was even created.' 'Are they sons of Adam?,' they asked. He answered, 'They know not that Adam was even created.' Ibn ʿAbbās (may God be pleased with him) reported that the Messenger of God (may God bless him and grant him peace) said, 'God has a white land, over which the sun passes in the course of thirty days of our world. It is filled with creatures of God who do not know that God is disobeyed on earth, nor that God created Adam and the Devil.' Ghazālī mentions all this in *Jawāhir al-Qur'ān*.

In summary, to say that this planet is the only world is nothing but an attempt to usurp God's authority, and is a statement completely devoid of knowledge. I compiled a book on this subject and entitled it *Miftāḥ al-shuhūd fī maẓāhir al-wujūd* ('The Key of Witnessing: on the Phenomena of Existence'); consult it, for the wonders of the age are contained within it.

The Compassionate, the Merciful [Q.1.3]

They are two Names, the former universal and the latter restricted. We say that the former is universal in that it encompasses every kind of favour: every favour which is perceived instinctively, and which the individual attributes to himself, is actually an effect of the Compassionate; and all that is subtle and imperceptible is an effect of the Merciful. We say that the latter is restricted in that it it belongs to

Him alone and cannot be acquired by another, save for those through whom He works it, 'The merciful are shown mercy by God.'[1]

SPIRITUAL: The word *Raḥīm* has an intensiveness to it that *Raḥmān* does not; for He [*al-Raḥīm*] is all the more tender with particulars, and all the more pitying of the state of servanthood (*ᶜubūdiyya*). He sends His emanations of mercy as they are required. The spirit of mercy is kind to the elderly, and compassionate to the young; it is adorned with humility, and available to all who seek it; it gives water to the thirsty, consoles the grief-stricken, feeds the hungry, leads the blind, comforts the estranged, visits the sick. Were you to see it, you would feel pity for it. This is especially true at the furthest end of manifestation[2] at the final moment of birth, bringing out the newborn from the womb.

King of the Day of Judgement [Q.1.4]

EXEGETICAL: That is, the Day of Requital (*yawm al-jazā'*), wherein each soul will be given that which it has earned. Were it not that He mentions this sentence right after *the Compassionate, the Merciful*, we would not have sought refuge in

You we worship, and from You we seek help [Q.1.5]

ALLEGORICAL: His words *You we worship and from You we seek help* inspire in us a consciousness of the necessary link between the Law and the Truth.[3] The first half of the verse is the Law and the second is the Truth; the first affirms an element of acquisition, and the second negates it; the first is closer to the common perception and the second is more preferable to the elite; this is because the first entails acting *for* God, while the second entails acting *by* God. The first is the act of the pious (*abrār*), because they act for the sake of God; the second is the act of those-brought-nigh (*muqarrabūn*), because they subsist

1 *Ḥadīth*.
2 The physical form is the culmination of manifestation.
3 Two of the elements of the common Sufi ternary: the Law (*sharīᶜa*), the Way (*ṭarīqa*) and the Truth (*ḥaqīqa*).

in God. The goal of the first is to seek reward, while the second is its own reward; this is because the first is concerned with fulfilling religious obligations, whilst the second is concerned with the fruits of gnosis. The first half is strenuous effort; the second, witnessing. One endures the pains of his worship; the other enjoys the delights of his vision. *Unto each do We extend, these and those, from your Lord's bounty* [Q.XVII.20].

Worship is mentioned before the seeking of help due to the perspective of the masses, which is to view the action before its outcome; the perspective of the elite, on the other hand, is to view it [i.e. worship] afterward, since they are so absorbed in beholding the outcome that they do not see the action. The former seek the help of acts of worship to reach Him, while the latter seek help from Him to perform acts of worship, as [for them] He is the one who acts and there is no other.

The wording of the verse brings the pronouns of the Object and subjects of worship together, which is effected by delaying the verb: *You we worship*.[1] This serves to inspire in the worshipper a consciousness of how close he is to God in principle, whatever he may have felt his position in relation to God was prior to the acts of worship coming into being. Worship, then, is not the means by which proximity is attained; this is why the Prophet (may God bless him and grant him peace) said, 'None of you shall enter Paradise by his works.' This means that the worshipper exists before the worship. Hence gnosis comes before worship; it is gnosis that makes worship necessary, and not the other way round.

Concerning the shift from the third to the second person; that is, from *Praise be to God* to *You we worship*, this teaches the aspirant how his journey will end, taking him from absence from God to presence with Him, until all intermediaries are removed and it becomes a direct discourse between the two parties: *You we worship, and from You we seek help*, and no other.

1 In the Arabic, '*You we*' is one word: *Iyyāka*.

SPIRITUAL: The 'we' of *You we worship* is annihilated in that of *from You we seek help*, so that when the worship is limited to the seeking of help, there remain the seeking of help and the Helper; what, then, becomes of the worship and the worshipper? If you are possessed of true certainty, you will see that his [i.e. the worshipper's] innermost secret heart (*sirr*) worships Him, while his reality (*ḥaqīqa*) beholds Him. He who [only] says *You we worship* does not know God, and he who [only] says *from You we seek help* does not worship Him.[1]

Guide us upon the straight path [Q.I.6]

EXEGETICAL: Guidance is of several kinds. The word expresses a faculty that acts in man and in other animals as well, alerting each to the presence of benefits and harms, according to aptitude. In the case of man, it has two halves: the lower half pertains to the animal realm, the higher half to the angelic realm; and the latter is what is intended here. In addition, human guidance is of [a further] two types: there are those whom God guides, and there are those whom He increases in guidance. The one *whose breast God expands for surrender to Him* [Q.XXXIX.22], by placing him on the straight path that leads to Paradise, has been guided; as for the one whom He increases in guidance, he is the one to whom He alludes by saying *God guides to His light whom He will* [Q.XXIV.35].

The *straight path* alludes to a prophetic law and a heavenly way, from the perspective of practical worship. From the perspective of intellectual (or we might say doctrinal) worship, it alludes to a middle way between two extremes, those of negligence and excess. Thus it is the most difficult thing to perceive, and cannot be traversed alone, even by someone with great spiritual aptitude. Many stand upon it, but few traverse it, and even fewer reach the destination.

SPIRITUAL: I asked one who is a reference [in such matters][2] about 'the path of the intellect' (*ṣirāṭ al-ʿuqūl*), and he answered, 'It is a fine line and

1 The Shaykh al-ʿAlawī says in his *Ḥikam* (Aphorisms): 'Whoso knows God does not worship Him; only his innermost secret heart worships Him.' (see Shaykh al-ʿAlawī's *Dīwān*, p. 143, Beirut: Dār al-Kutub al-ʿIlmiyya, 2006).

2 That is, a spiritual master or gnostic saint.

a narrow path, difficult to traverse, full of obstacles; it passes between companionship and isolation at its onset, between divine incomparability (*tanzīh*) and analogy (*tashbīh*) in its middle, and between freedom (*ḥurriyya*) and obligation (*taklīf*)[1] at its end. To incline to either side is damaging, and to combine the two is impossible—save for the one who has two wings, and can embody two in one.' I said, 'How difficult it is to attain this!' and regretted ever asking.

The path of those upon whom is Your grace, not of those upon whom is wrath, nor those who are astray [Q.1.7]

EXEGESIS: The purpose of this sentence is to define the aforementioned path; the same path is described here by means of those upon it, and a warning is issued against inclining to either side of it, wherein are those upon whom is wrath, and those who are astray. Now those who stray from the path have a better chance of returning to it than those who incur wrath; this can be inferred from the fact that those who are astray are not those upon whom is wrath; rather, they are in the wilderness, until God takes them by the hand. Those upon whom is wrath are they who know full well what the path is, but decline to traverse it, and who know full well what the truth is but refuse to follow it. Do you not see that He attributes the straying to them, but the wrath to Himself? Those who incur God's wrath are in far greater peril than those who stray from His path—and we seek His refuge from them both!

JURIDICAL: From His words *Praise be to God* up to *nor those who are astray*, twelve rulings can be deduced: Firstly, we learn that there is no swifter way to earn God's goodly acceptance than to acknowledge His favours. He indicated this by placing the invocation of praise at the very start of the Book.

Secondly, we learn that God acknowledges His servant's status as a subject of His lordship, even if the servant does not recognise this lord-

1 *Taklīf* is a legal term for the religious obligations applicable to all adult Muslims. Thus, according to the above quotation, the end of the 'path of intellect' is a balance between legal obligation and spiritual freedom.

ship; thus He says *Lord of the worlds*, thereby making all the inhabitants of the world equal in this subject-Lord relationship.

Thirdly, we learn that there are worlds beyond count, since He refers to them in the plural.

Fourthly, we learn that the divine Beauty has precedence over the divine Majesty, since the Names 'the Compassionate' and 'the Merciful' are mentioned before any other Names.

Fifthly, we learn from His word *King of the Day of Judgement* that on the Day of Requital, God will manifest only with the Quality of Justice, not with either Beauty alone or Majesty alone.

Sixthly, we learn from His words *You we worship and from You we seek help* that Islam has two halves, one pertaining to Law and the other to Truth.

Seventhly, we learn from His placing *You we worship* before *from You we seek help* that the aspirant usually does not attain to the Truth until he has first expended his effort in fulfilling his obligations.

Eighthly, we learn from His use of the plural pronoun 'we' in *we worship* that it is preferred to offer the five daily prayers in congregation, since the context is one of humility, where it would not be fitting for an individual to magnify himself by saying 'we'.

Ninthly, we learn from His words *You we worship and from You we seek help* that prayer is a time of intimate discourse, when we address God directly.

Tenthly, we learn that the most important thing to ask of God is guidance to the straight path.

Eleventhly, we learn that God wants us to raise our aspirations by asking Him for the highest stations, not the lowest. We can infer this from His words *The path of those upon whom is Your grace*, since this clearly includes the prophets, the most sincere, the martyrs and the righteous.[1]

1 Allusion to Qur'ānic verse IV.69: *Whoever obeys God and the messenger, they are with those to whom God has shown favour, of the prophets and the most sincere and the martyrs and the righteous.*

Twelfthly, we learn that those upon whom there is wrath are lower than those who are astray, which is why they are mentioned first.

ALLEGORICAL: God's command that we ask Him for the path of those who are given grace, namely the prophets, the most sincere, the martyrs and righteous, provides encouragement and motivation for seeking the highest stations. It also affirms that the stations of the spiritual elite are still accessible, and were not only the province of those who lived in ages past; as long as this *Sūra* can still be recited, it is still possible to request the path of those who are given grace, and to traverse it to its destination. The prophethood of the Prophet is no longer possible to attain, but his sainthood (*wilāya*) may still be inherited.

Amen[1]

EXEGETICAL: 'Amen' is a noun performing the function of a verb; it means 'Answer!' The Messenger of God (may God bless him and grant him peace) said, 'Gabriel taught me to say *Amen* when I finish reciting the Opening of the Book, and said it is the equivalent of reciting the entire Book.' Wā'il b. Ḥajar[2] (may God be pleased with him) reported that whenever the Prophet (may God bless him and grant him peace) recited *Nor those who are astray*, he would say *Amen* with a loud voice. All are agreed that it is not actually part of the Qur'ān, which means that to say it after the *Fātiḥā* is a *Sunna* action. There is a difference of opinion about whether the imam in prayer should say it out loud; but it seems to us that he should, since the above *ḥadīth* stipulates that it was said out loud.

ALLEGORICAL COMMENTARY ON THE *SŪRA* AS A WHOLE: That the *Fātiḥa* begins with the Holy Name and ends with *Nor those who are astray* is a sign for those who would behold it. The Supreme Name[3] (*al-Ism al-Aʿẓam*) comes at its head to symbolise how He is at the summit of all the realities it contains, both those pertaining to the Real and those

1 The Shaykh here gives a commentary on the word *Āmīn* ('Amen', 'let it be so'), which is usually pronounced after the *Fātiḥā*.

2 A Companion of the Prophet.

3 The Supreme Name refers to *Allāh*.

pertaining to creation. From this most complete manifestation, there is then a hierarchical descent through the levels of the outward and the inward, until the Real is completely hidden at the furthermost point of *those upon whom is wrath* and *those who are astray*, where He is scarcely known at all, and where *sight does not overtake Him* [Q.VI.103].

A tradition states that the *Fātiḥa* is split between the servant and his Lord. The servant's share is the lower half; for just as lordship implies outward manifestation, servitude implies inward seclusion. His Names are given in the upper half as signs of outward manifestation: *God* (*Allāh*), *Lord* (*Rabb*), *the Compassionate* (*al-Raḥmān*), *the Merciful* (*al-Raḥīm*), *the King* (*al-Malik*); these five are all outwardly apparent. Then in the lower half, He speaks of Himself again five times, each of them indirect and hidden: there is the second person pronoun in *You we worship*, and again in *from You we seek help*; then the elided subject pronoun of *Guide us*; then the second person pronoun in *Your grace*; and finally the implicit pronoun in *upon whom is* [*Your*] *wrath*. These are five of His Names, all of them indirect and hidden, in contrast to the five which are outwardly apparent; so there is consonance and balance. Thus it is clear that He is the Outwardly Manifest in all that is outward, and the Inwardly Hidden in all that is hidden; and in all cases, He is God: *He it is who is God in Heaven and God on earth* [Q.XLIII.84].

Know also that the Essence is directly followed in the descending hierarchy by the Quality of Lordship, which is why the Name 'Lord' is given directly after the Name of the Essence. Then comes the Quality of Compassion, because of its connection with the 'rising': *The Compassionate, raised upon the Throne* [Q.XX.5]; since when the 'worlds' are mentioned, this 'rising' becomes relevant. Then comes the Quality of Mercy for all who are 'risen' upon, thus proclaiming their equality; and then comes Kingship, to judge between them when they differ. Now when the Lordship reaches this point in the hierarchical descent, namely that of judgement between the servants, the inevitable consequence is that the station of servitude attaches to it and says, *You we worship, and from You we seek help*. Once this recourse has been made in the right way, He speaks of Himself indirectly, since the context is now that of inwardness, although the pronoun which indicates Him is mentioned first: *You we worship, and from You we seek help*. He then hides Himself even further, so that the pronoun which indicates Him is delayed: *Guide us to the straight path, the path of those upon whom is Your grace*. He disappears completely in *those upon whom is wrath*, where there is no pronoun at all, but only an implicit understanding that the wrath is His. Finally, He absents Himself entirely from *nor those who are astray*; though in reality they are objects, He makes them subjects. This is the absolute limit of disappearance; yet for the folk of true clarity, it is really pure manifestation.

SPIRITUAL: [This perspective] does not see the first word of the *Fātiḥā*, 'praise', as separate from what follows it; it sees that the *Fātiḥa* itself, and all that is in it, belongs to God; otherwise we could not say 'Praise be to God', since one of the names of the *Fātiḥa* is 'Praise', and this belongs to God.[1]

1 One of the traditional names of the *Fātiḥa* is *al-Ḥamd*, 'Praise'; the Shaykh therefore reasons that since the *Sūra* begins 'Praise be to God,' it is itself dedicated to God by these words, and so on in an infinite circle.

The Kernel of Knowledge on the Chapter of the Star[1]

In the Name of God, the Compassionate, the Merciful

Praise be to Him who made to gush forth from the hearts of His Friends a spring of His well-guarded secret, thus causing to flow from their lips that which gives joy to the soul; and then He drew our gaze to this, according to His words, *Ask, then, the people of remembrance, if ye know not* [Q.XVI.43], so that the hearts of men flocked to their circles, that they might be granted to see that which had been veiled from them; and the clouds of mercy rained upon them, and the suns of gnosis and the moons of wisdom rose above them, and they drew from this enough to suffice all of the worlds, and then returned to us, exclaiming: *Blessed, then, is God, the best of creators!* [Q.XXIII.14].

You asked us, O beloved—may God grant us and you a good end!—to produce an exegesis of the Noble Qur'ān according to the method of the men of special understanding and sound experience (*dhawq*)[2]. What you requested would not be impossible, were there but time to do it. In any case, by way of granting your request, I began to consider what part of the Qur'ān I might restrict myself to, after having first purified myself of my own understanding[3] and detached myself from my own conjecture. The Chapter of 'The Star' (*al-Najm*) came to me, and I dove into its midst, and delved into its secrets, and it became clear to me that I could spend much time swimming in its oceans, so I said, 'God is my sufficiency, and the best of

1 *Lubāb al-ilm fī sūrat wa'l-Najm*. Mostaghanem: al-Maṭbaʿa al-ʿAlāwiyya, n.d.
2 The Sufis often refer to their experiential knowledge as being *dhawq*, 'taste'.
3 That is, in deference to inspiration from God.

trustees, and in Him is all aid sought!' And I named the result: *The Kernel of Knowledge on the Chapter of the Star.*

The Almighty says:

In the Name of God, the Compassionate, the Merciful.
By the star when it sets [Q.LIII.1]

The opening of this noble Chapter with the word *star* tells us that something of great importance is to be expounded; for a star rises and sets, ascends and descends, and therefore it is full of wondrous mysteries. If the one who hears these words reflects on the setting of a star and how, despite its enormous size and high position, it sets and then rises again, he will not be incredulous when he hears how the Prophet ascended to the heavens, and how Gabriel descended to earth—may peace be upon them both! Rather he will see this as perfectly possible and well within the power of the Almighty, and he will assert that this is an aspect of God's way with His prophets: when each is ready for the ascension, He takes him up; and this is part of the nature which He has given them. He said of the Prophet Idrīs, *We raised him to a high place* [Q.XIX.57], and of Jesus, *Nay, God raised him to Himself* [Q.IV.158]. The same was the case with Muḥammad (may God bless him and grant him peace) save that Muḥammad then returned to complete his mission: he returned in body, but not in spirit, for his spirit never departed the Highest Assembly. The Prophet said in this regard, 'I spend my nights with my Lord, who feeds me and gives me to drink.' This refers to his spirit, whilst his body remained on earth in its usual state.

Moreover, I say that the purpose of this oath[1] is to symbolizes a brilliant light which is the source of all lights, and the foundation of all vision and all insight; this refers to nothing else save the Muḥammadan Soul (*al-nafs al-Muḥammadiyya*) and the Eternal Spirit (*al-rūḥ al-abadiyya*); and every man partakes in this to the extent he

1 I.e. the words at the beginning of the Chapter: *By the star*...

aspires to, and every heart may contain as much of this as it can bear.

God says: *By the star when it sets*. The basis of the symbolism which exists between the star and the Muḥammadan Soul is that each one of them is a source of guidance. In addition, they are united in the light which they emit. The meaning of this is that a star can be used as a guide because of how it sets and rises; were it not for this motion, it would not be a source of guidance, for its shifting and its motion are necessary for guidance. The same is true for the Muḥammadan Soul: it guides because of how it moves away from its highest position, turning away from the Divine Realities in order to fulfil those human functions which are necessary for it, so that it may become a model and a guide for those who seek guidance.[1]

Because of this, every time we see an instance where the Prophet's soul inclined towards something, we must be aware that this inclination embodies many wise lessons and beneficial mysteries which may be comprehensible to those who have knowledge—and the one who knows is not like the one who knows not. We must be careful not to imagine that his inclination towards anything was simply the result of human nature and personal choice, which would imply a deviation from the path of righteousness and transcendence. No, for He who knows all that is secret has said:

Your companion has erred not, nor has he strayed [Q.LIII.2]

That is, he did not err when he was kept, by those things in which he had to engage, from that which was the purpose of his creation, namely to occupy himself with God and turn solely to Him. This means that his actions were not based on human nature like those of others, but rather it is as he said, 'Three things of your world have been made beloved to me.' He did not say, 'I love,' thereby ascribing the action to himself; the one possessed of insight may therefore see that he was compelled in this matter and not free. In the company

1 That is, the coming of a divine Messenger to earth to live amongst men is a kind of sacrifice on his part.

of men he was yet in the company of the Real; the one did not veil him from the other. *Each one has a direction to which he turns his face* [Q.II.148].

And it would have been inappropriate for him to speak in front of men about the nature of the state he realized when he was in the company of the Real, and therefore God says:

Nor does he speak of passion[1] [Q.LIII.3]

The first thing one understands from this is that he does not simply invent the Qur'ān of his own passion, or more generally that he does not perform any action, whether openly or secretly, save that God Almighty is the One who acts through him, *You threw not, when you threw, but God it was that threw* [Q.VIII.17]. In this regard, God says, *See by Him, and hear!* [Q.XVIII.26].[2]

I say, however, that the best way to explain the word 'passion' (*hawā*) here is to say that it means 'love' (*maḥabba*), and that therefore the words 'Nor does he speak of passion' mean: Nor does he speak of the secrets of love which his heart contains, and with which he has been singled out above all mankind such that there are few who could bear them. It has even been said that God's words *God's burning fire, which overcomes the hearts* [Q.CIV.6–7] refer to love, and that His words *Lord, burden us not with that which is beyond our strength* [Q.II.286] means the love which is too much for a man to bear. The Prophet had an immense share of this love, to the extent that he was called *al-Ḥabīb*, 'the Beloved'. Yet he did not do anything to display any yearning he felt, because to love means to keep the secrets of one's beloved. Even if he had been instructed to reveal that which his heart concealed, most would not have been able to understand it or accept

1 The word *hawā* has several meanings; usually here it is be rendered 'desire' or 'wish', but based on the Shaykh al-ʿAlawī's commentary it has been rendered 'passion'.

2 This translation attempts to capture the Shaykh al-ʿAlawī's esoteric interpretation of the words *abṣir bihi wa-asmiʿ*, which might ordinarily be translated as 'See how well He hears and sees!'

it, for people have become accustomed to antipathy and avoidance of what matters most, unless they are reconnected with and reattached to the mediator [the Prophet]. Thus He says:

It is naught but revelation being revealed [Q.LIII.4]

That is, it is not easy to speak of it. Someone said of this:

The Lovers share a secret which cannot be told
By any words, nor any deeds, of man.

Jesus (peace be upon him) attained to the same illuminations of the Divine Presence (*al-Ḥaḍra al-Ilāhiyya*) and wonders of the heart as did Muḥammad, yet Muḥammad was better able to keep these secrets than was any other. He did not reveal anything which might cause confusion in the minds of men, for God taught him how to keep these secrets to himself, as He says:

One of mighty powers did teach him, One vigorous! [Q.LIII.5-6]

That is, the Steadfastly Strong (*al-Qawiyy al-Matīn*) taught him, for vigour means steadfastness and strength; and this was required so that Muḥammad in turn would be steadfast and strong enough to bear the mysteries imparted to him—praise meted out to a teacher is meted out in turn to the teacher's pupil. Therefore he would only reveal such things to those who were worthy. One of his Companions once asked him, 'Should I convey all that I hear from you, O Messenger of God?' He replied, 'All but those words which are beyond the minds of common people, and which would thus cause mischief among them.' And because of this, the Companions are not known to have said things which some minds cannot comprehend, unlike other great men, who said many things which require much interpretation. This was also true of the words of Christ (peace be upon him) such that even the Apostles were usually unable to decipher his words until he explained them himself. Those who understand these sayings in a literal sense, without taking the trouble to interpret them correctly, will see in them evidence for his divinity. One example of this is how the Gospel reports—if it has not been altered in any way—that he said to the gathered people: 'You are from beneath; I am from above: you are of this world; I am not of this world.' [John 8:23] He also said in the Gospel, 'I and my Father are one.' [John 10:30] And he said to those who challenged him with, 'Show us the Father':

> He that has seen me has seen the Father; and how say you, Show us the Father? Believe you not that I am in the Father, and the Father in me? The words that I speak unto you I speak not of myself: but the Father that dwells in me, he does the works. [John 14:9-10]

If these words are truly the words of Christ, they require interpretation and commentary, just as some of the statements of the gnostics require the same; for to understand them literally would be harmful to ordinary people, and to reject them would be even worse, for they are not without wisdom which the wise can understand. Because of this, Muḥammad (may God bless him and grant him peace) was unique in that he did not force his followers to decipher that which is nigh indecipherable, but rather he would convey to each of them according to his capacity for things divine, because intellects are at different levels, and mysteries are each unique, as the Prophet said, 'Speak to people at their intellectual level. Do you want them to deny God and His messenger?' By so doing, he did the people a great kindness. This is why Jesus said towards the end of the Gospel, alluding to his coming:

> I have yet many things to say to you: but you cannot bear them now. Howbeit when he, the Spirit of truth, is come, he will guide you into all truth: for he shall not speak of himself; but whatsoever he shall hear, [that] shall he speak: and he will show you things to come. He shall glorify me: for he shall receive of mine, and shall show [it] unto you. [John 16:12-14]

Praise be to God, these glad tidings of Christ bring together many of the Prophet's attributes—may peace and blessings be upon him!

The Almighty then says:

And He grew clear to view, when He was on the uppermost horizon [Q.LIII.6–7]

The pronoun 'He' in *He grew clear to view* refers to *One of mighty powers*; and His words *on the uppermost horizon* speak of a special condition and a transcendent rank, free of any suspicion of comparison or addition[1]—it [the transcendent rank] does not refer to the entirety of His Essence, but only to one of His 'faces': *Each one has a direction to which he turns his face* [Q.II.148]. And there are countless faces, and infinite attributes, by means of which the Real comes down to His loved ones and His elect, so that their knowledge of Him can become complete. For them to perceive Him in this way is impossible unless He 'comes down' to them, just as He 'came down' to Muḥammad.

Then He drew nigh, and came down [Q.LIII.8]

He did so in a metaphysical sense, not a physical one, for it is impossible that He could 'move', or be 'separate' or 'attached'. Likewise, His words *came down* refer to a metaphysical 'descent', not a literal one.

Till He was but two bows' nigh, or nearer [Q.LIII.9]

Two bows' nigh signifies ultimate proximity, and *or nearer* means that He was even nearer than that, such that the Prophet was so completely immersed in this nearness he was cognizant of nothing else. And had the Almighty not come down and descended, Muḥammad would not have been able to know Him with such intimacy when He was on the uppermost horizon. It is impossible to perceive His innermost Essence (*kunhiyya*) in any way unless He assents to come down to one, whereupon one may perceive him according to the knowledge that one possesses; and one can only perceive Him in creation, because the individual is part of creation. What this means is that He is only

1 The Shaykh al-ʿAlawī considers these words to refer to God, not the angel Gabriel as most commentators opine; therefore he takes special care here to affirm the symbolic and essential mystical nature of this passage.

revealed in the mirror of created beings.[1] He is already plainly manifested before this, but the individual must discover this manifestation, whereupon he exclaims, 'I have seen the Real in creation!' Thus the Prophet (may God bless him and grant him peace) said, 'I saw my Lord in the form of a beardless young man.' He also said, 'I never saw anything save that I saw God within it.' And Abraham said of the star, *This is my Lord!* [Q.VI.76]. Jesus saw Him in his own self, and thus said, 'I and the Father are one' [John 10:30], and 'He that has seen me has seen the Father' [John 14:9], and so on. And the truth of the matter is beyond all of this, but this is as far as human understanding can go, and therefore you must accept this. In reality, all things are perishing,[2] and the truth of the matter cannot be expressed more than this, for were His Qualities to be fully revealed all His creation would be annihilated.

And speaking of how the Prophet was completely enfolded in the Being of his Maker, God says:

And He revealed unto His servant that which He revealed [Q.LIII.10]

That He only alludes to what was revealed, instead of stating it plainly, indicates that it is something which cannot be easily expressed. The meaning is that it was greater than anything which the mind can imagine, and that it was not simple words of command and prohibition, but was something which grasped the heart and imparted a great mystery unto it. This is explained by what follows:

The heart lied not of what it saw [Q.LIII.11]

The revelation here came through a state of grasping nearness and direct contact; a state that is shrouded in mystery and cannot be conveyed by any means other than direct experience, for words cannot express it, even the words of 'he who was vouchsafed the

1 The Shaykh al-ʿAlawī says in one of his poems: 'The universe for Him is a mirror, and a locus for His Qualities' (*lahu al-kawnu mir'āt, wa-maẓhar al-ṣifāt*). *Dīwān*, (Beirut: Dār al-Kutub al-ʿIlmiyya, 2006), p. 63.

2 Reference to *All things are perishing, save for His face* (Q.XXVIII.88).

compendium of speech.'[1] Indeed he did express it in a way which could be understood,[2] yet even so many hard-hearted people refused to believe it, denying it as others had denied similar things of old. The Almighty thus rebuked them, saying:

Will you, then, dispute with him what he sees? [Q.LIII.12]

That is, will you argue with him and object to him because of the grandeur and majesty which was revealed to him? It would have been more fitting for you to have refrained from objecting to the true vision of which he informed you, for the heart sees what the eye cannot. And how would you react if he told you of the divine Qualities and Names which he witnessed with his very eyes? *Then whosoever will, let him believe, and whosoever will, let him disbelieve* [Q.XVIII.29].

Indeed, he saw Him at another descent, by the Lote-tree of the uttermost end [Q.LIII.13–14]

This means he saw Him on another occasion. God uses the word 'descent' (*nazla*) to express again how He 'came down,' because this vision was sensory (*fī 'l-ḥiss*) whereas the one before it had been only spiritual (*fī 'l-maʿnā*); and thus the Prophet experienced both kinds of vision, one inner and the other outer.

The 'Lote-tree of the uttermost end' means the Lote-tree which stood at the very end of the journey: *With your Lord is the uttermost end* [Q.LIII.42]. The 'Lote-tree' symbolises the very essence of the vision, and some express this by calling it the 'Universal Tree'.[3] The point of similarity between the Lote-tree and what we have mentioned is that the tree is composed of three elements: thorns, fruits, and leaves, just

1 This is one of the traditional names of the Prophet.
2 This implies that much of the Prophet's subsequent description of the Night Ascension was symbolic and metaphorical.
3 See Abū Bakr Sirāj ad-Dīn, *The Book of Certainty* (Islamic Texts Society: Cambridge, 1992), p. 14.

as all beings are divided into three classes.[1] *And God coins similitudes for men, that they may remember* [Q.XIV.25].

I say, moreover, that this vision was more precious than the one which preceded it, because of all the many singular elements it combined and brought together. It was too precious an experience to be granted to any but Muḥammad, save by means of inheritance—and 'The sages are the heirs of the prophets.' Thus the Almighty then says:

Whereby is the Garden of Refuge [Q.LIII.15]

This means the ultimate end of the experiential knowledge of God which is possible; when a person reaches it, the lights of the divine Presence envelop him—nay, they envelop the entire world, so that he does not see anything without seeing God therein, as the Prophet had said. This is the meaning of:

When there enshrouded the Lote-tree That
which enshrouds [Q.LIII.16]

That is, it was covered and enveloped by divine illuminations, until it was entirely removed from all other beings, whatever their rank, whether majestic or lowly, basking in the glow of the light of God's Names and Qualities: *God is the light of the heavens and the earth* [Q.XXIV.35]. And because of this last theophany, which God called the 'other descent', Muḥammad was able to see with his very eyes, and not only with his heart as he had before; his eyesight (*baṣar*) became one with his insight (*baṣīra*),[2] and therefore God praised him by saying:

The eye swerved not, nor did it stray! [Q.LIII.17]

The eyesight did not waver from what the insight beheld; *nor did it stray*, meaning that it did not go beyond or away from that wherein

1 This is an allusion to *And you will be three classes* (Q.LVI.7), referring to the three possible states of the afterlife: the foremost, the people of the right, and the people of the left. See Martin Lings, *A Return to the Spirit* (Fons Vitae: Louisville, 2005), p. 64.

2 The *baṣīra* is the sight of the 'inner eye', or the 'eye of the heart' (*ʿayn al-qalb*).

the Real manifested Itself, but rather paid full attention to It. The Prophet knew his Lord better than anyone, and he never missed any of His theophanies no matter how it appeared or occurred. The upshot of this is that Muḥammad experienced the two visions simultaneously: that of the heart and that of the eye. God said of the former, *The heart lied not of what it saw* [Q.LIII.11], and of the latter: *The eye swerved not, nor did it stray!* [Q.LIII.17]. And the Prophet himself said, 'I saw my Lord with my eye, and with my heart.'

Moreover, know that no outward eye can see the Real, in any way, unless its sight reflects that of the inward eye, just as the Prophet's outer eye reflected and was at one with his inner eye. Ismāʿīl Ḥaqqī al-Barūsī says in *Rūḥ al-bayān*, citing *al-Ta'wīlāt al-najmiyya*[1] that the Prophet's inner eye was united with his outer eye, so that he saw with his inner eye the inwardness of the Real insomuch as He is the Inwardly Hidden (*al-Bāṭin*), and he saw with his outer eye the outwardness of the Real inasmuch as He is the Outwardly Manifest (*al-Ẓāhir*); and it is obvious that the outward can only be seen by the outward, and that the inward can only be seen by the inward.

If you ask why no one but the Prophet (may God bless him and grant him peace) can partake of the direct vision of God in this world, although nothing can come between the eye and His outward manifestation; and if you ask why the Prophet was singled out alone for this, I say: This is not because the Supreme Essence cannot be seen; it is because no eye possesses the ability to see It. This is why one of the great saints said that all that prevents the Real from being seen in this world is that people do not recognise Him; they can see but they do not see Him: they do not know that what they are seeing is the Real. Thus they are veiled from Him by their own obtuseness, nothing more. The reason why the Prophet was able to see what no other could see was that his intellectual penetration (*faṭāna*) was more perfect than theirs, for he knew with certitude that the eye does not fall upon what is inexistent, and thus whatever the eyes fall upon

1 By Aḥmad al-Sanānī (d. 1336).

must have the Real manifested in it, for in themselves all things are nothingness. Because of this, he was able to partake of the vision of the eye (*al-ruʿya al-baṣariyya*); and he who has the slightest share of the prophetic penetration will not be denied his own share of God's manifest presence in all things.

After all this, I say that the vision of the heart (*al-ruʿya al-qalbiyya*) has a closer bond to the Real than the vision of the eye. For it would be impossible for the latter to combine and integrate all the separate entities and divergent elements were it not that the world is immersed in the lights of divine Unity which burn forth from the tree of *Wheresoever you turn, there is the face of God* [Q.II.115]. Whoever attains this goal has reached the end beyond which there is no passing, and God speaks of Muḥammad's reaching it by saying:

> *Verily he beheld, of all the signs of his Lord, the Greatest* [Q.LIII.18]

Know that this sign is not the same sign of which God said *That We might show him of Our signs* [Q.XVII.1], for here it is called the *Greatest* sign. This gives us the sense that this sign was not a created thing, nor even a theophany of the divine Names and Qualities; it was nothing less than a vision of the lights of the Holy Essence. And so it is called the *Greatest*. The Prophet held this state dearer to him than any other, and said of it, 'I have moments when nothing suffices me but my Lord.' And he also said, 'O Lord, increase me in marvelling at You!' Were the sign anything other than the vision, it would have had to be greater than [the vision], since God calls it the *Greatest*: and indeed, *God's goodly acceptance* (riḍwān) *is greater* [Q.IX.72].

You should be aware that what we have spoken of, namely the possibility of the outward eye beholding the Real, will seem very far-fetched to many people, even those who claim to have knowledge, and they may even say that such a thing is impossible both rationally and scripturally. The Muʿtazila were of this opinion, and they were satisfied that this was necessary because of the consideration that in order for the eye to see something, this thing must be confined to a physical space. Yet it did not occur to them that this in turn would deny that God's sight can fall upon created beings, on the grounds that in doing so His sight would be confined to the location of the object seen. And we would thus have to conclude that God has no perception—how far exalted is He above this! Success here lies with those who give this matter over to those who truly understand it, for it is too mysterious for every mind to comprehend. God says, *Do not pursue that of which you have no knowledge; the hearing, the sight, the heart—you will be questioned about all of these* [Q.XVII.36]. So the sight becomes questionable whenever it falls upon anything but God; and likewise the hearing becomes questionable when it hears anything from anyone but God, and so does the heart when it gives thought to anything but God. Someone said in this regard:

> If, but for a forgetful moment, desire for any but You
> Came flitting to my mind, I would judge me an apostate.

And the Real—glory be to Him!—now rebukes anyone whose sight falls upon anything but Him, saying with word of censure:

> *Have you seen, then, al-Lāt and al-ʿUzzā,*
> *And Manāt the third, the other?* [Q.LIII.19-20][1]

That is: You find cause to deny that Muḥammad experienced this unveiling of precious realities, when in fact the sight truly should never see anything else. Why, then, do you not censure yourselves for what your eyes have seen, and what your hearts have desired, of these possible beings which do not even truly exist and which are nothing more than illusions and imaginary shapes that say to the intelligent person, through their very states: *We are but a temptation; do not, then, disbelieve!* [Q.II.102]. Is it not curious that you rely on such possible beings and count on them to the point that you even make gods of them? Your gaze is fixed on them and you come to see al-Lāt, and al-ʿUzzā, and Manāt the third, the other, and many other things

1 Al-Lāt, al-ʿUzzā and Manāt were chief among the idols of Quraysh. See Lings, *Muhammad*, p. 15.

which contradict the Oneness of the Essence, such as means (*ʿilal*), causes (*asbāb*), and intermediaries (*wasā'iṭ*). And you come to trust in yourselves more than you trust in God, Who says:

What, have you males, and He females?
That were indeed an unjust division [Q.LIII.21-22]

That is, your division is wrong and unfair, for you have claimed for yourselves more than you allow for God; for what share have you in the holy Names and the divine actions? Thus your error is grave indeed; and this means that all you have seen, and all you have relied upon, is bereft of any reality.

They are but names you have named—you and your fathers;
God has sent down no authority for them [Q.LIII.23]

You have no reliable proof that they have any effect on existence, or that they even partake in it.

They follow naught but surmise, and what the souls desire [Q.LIII.23]

And it is obvious that the soul desires only the illusions which conform to it, for its own existence is illusory, and *surmise avails naught against truth* [Q.LIII.28].

I say, moreover, that the instinctive nature of the soul is to refuse to surrender to anything, even to the Truth, and therefore it opposes that element of the divine Unity which would imply its own effacement, and resists it any way it can, even if this means affirming the role of intermediate means and causality, albeit only metaphorically. It does this out of jealousy;[1] and when it is presented with the notion of true Unity, which affirms that all of creation is non-existent, and that God is the only true Being in Essence, Qualities and Deeds, the soul turns away, saying, *We heard this not from our forefathers of old!* [Q.XXIII.24]. This is because for the soul to affirm such a thing would

1 The Shaykh al-ʿAlawī is alluding to the Qur'ānic verse I.109 though the verse itself refers to the unbelievers and their jealousy of the believers. The meaning here is that the soul is jealously protective of its own existence.

be to wipe itself from the slate of existence, and therefore it shudders at the mere mention of pure Unity: *When God is mentioned alone, then shudder the hearts of those who believe not in the hereafter; yet when those besides Him are mentioned, lo! they rejoice* [Q.XXXIX.45]. This is plain to see, and can be found in every 'soul which enjoins evil'.[1]

And yet guidance has come to them from their Lord! [Q.LIII:23]

But it only guides those who follow it: *And many a sign there is in the heavens and the earth which they pass by, turning away from it* [Q.XII.105]. The sacred scriptures and prophetic sayings contain many allusions to the doctrine of pure Unity, but some souls prefer to cling to the ground[2] and adhere to notions of multiplicity. Yet in God's words *Wheresoever you turn, there is the face of God* [Q.II.115], and *He is the First and the Last and the Outward and the Inward* [Q.LVII.3], is there not enough to erase all traces of anything other than Him? And consider His words *See by Him, and hear!* [Q.XVIII.26],[3] and *God is the light of the heavens and the earth* [Q.XXIV.35], and the words of the Prophet, 'Were you to lower a rope down as far as the seventh earth, you would come upon God,' and other sayings, all of which give us a sense of how the Almighty encompasses all things in their very essences—there is only He, and nothing else. Thus the messengers would allude to the doctrine of pure Unity in such as way as could be comprehended by those who heard them, *And of them some wrong themselves, some follow a middle course, and some are foremost in good works, by God's leave* [Q.XXXV.32]. All of this lest the soul say, *No tiding-bearer ever came to us* [Q.V.19], that is, 'no one ever came to tell us of the special station of knowledge'—God possesses the ultimate evidence against this. An instance of this is the argument Abraham presented to his people

1 Reference to the three stations of the soul in Islamic thought: the 'soul which enjoins evil', the 'self-reproaching soul', and the 'soul at peace'. See R. A. Nicholson, *Studies in Islamic Mysticism*, (Cambridge: Cambridge University Press, 1921), p. 110.

2 Allusion to Qur'ānic verse VII.176.

3 See note on this verse above.

when he saw a star and said, *This is my Lord* [Q.VI.76]; yet he found that people's hearts were not ready to receive these pure truths. So the Real consoled him and bade him not grieve for the shortcomings of his people, saying: *We raise the ranks of whomever We will* [Q.VI.83]. One of the gnostics said of this,

> Other things than You appeared to the eye
> That delighted in You, and I saw naught but You;
> Just as, before me, the Friend[1] looked above
> And turned his eyes to the firmament's stars.

All those who call to God by His leave [i.e. the messengers of God and the spiritual masters] do their best to gives proofs of His existence, so that the people have no complaint to raise with God once the messengers are gone. Let us allude to some instances of this. In the Book of Genesis, our master Jacob (peace be upon him) said, 'God Almighty appeared unto me at Luz in the land of Canaan,' [Genesis 48:3]. And the Book of Exodus states that God appeared to Moses in a flame of fire [Exodus 3:2-4], to which the Qur'ān alludes when it tells us that he said, *Verily, beyond all doubt I have seen a fire* [Q.XX.10]. And there is so much of this kind of language in the Gospel that it cannot all be quoted here, and there is plenty of it in the *Sunna* too. We only mentioned it here to show that the subtle allusions of those who came before us, whether the ancients or the more recent, point to what lies behind things, and that these were not created in vain, and that everything has its own ample share of God's manifestation in it—or through it. We must not restrict things to their outward appearances only; for if the sky were only the sky, and the earth were only the earth, and there were nothing more to them than that, then God would not have praised Abraham by saying, *And thus did We show Abraham the kingdom of the heavens and the earth, that he might be of those possessing certainty* [Q.VI.75]. Thus we see that there are secrets hidden

1 In Islam, Al-Khalīl or Khalīlu 'Llāh (the Friend or the Friend of God) is one of Abraham's names.

in the depths of things, to which God alludes by saying, *Say: Behold what is in the heavens and the earth!* [Q.x.101]. These words and others like them may guide the one who benefits from his knowledge to the truth that the Almighty is the one who *is aware of what every soul has earned* [Q.xiii.33].

One of the great saints of our time said that if you wish to rise above the level of those who require proofs and evidences of God, then repeat frequently, *He stands over every soul for what it has earned* (Q.xiii.33), and ask yourself if you can find anyone else who stands firm, self-sufficient and unchanging. Nay, you will find only people who are dying and being renewed at every instant. And once you have seen with your own eyes, there is no longer any need for proofs and evidence. *He is the First and the Last and the Outward and the Inward* [Q.lvii.3] at every moment; 'God was, and nothing was with Him,' and He is now as He ever was.[1]

So every allusion (*ishāra*) made by those who possess intimate knowledge of God contains guidance to the highest levels of spiritual excellence (*iḥsān*); but God guides whom He wills. And since the Almighty knows that the nature of the spiritual guide is to hope for all God's creatures to be guided—and in particular the Prophet hoped this for his community—He wants to remind these noble guides of how this [guidance] is dependent on the divine will and the particularities of the divine predestination, that they not become downhearted should their hopes be dashed. Therefore He says:

Or shall man have whatever he hopes for? [Q.liii.24]

That is, no man, whoever he may be, can have everything he hopes for unless it corresponds to the divine predestination; so let not your eagerness to guide others, O spiritual guide, obstruct your sincere resignation to the will of God. *If you can, seek out a hole in the earth, or*

1 Ibn ʿAṭā Allāh added this commentary to the *ḥadīth* in his *Ḥikam*, no. 37 in Danner's translation. Victor Danner, *The Book of Wisdom* (New York: Paulist Press, 1978), p. 55. It is often attributed to Imām ʿAlī, as in ʿAbd al-Qāhir al-Baghdādī, *al-Farq bayn al-firaq* (Beirut: Dār al-Āfāq al-Jadīda), 1971, p. 321.

a ladder in the sky, to bring them a sign; and had God willed, He would have brought them together in guidance [Q.VI.35]. Yet He did not will this, and had He brought them all to guidance, this would have contradicted the supreme wisdom which dictates that some must attain unto paradise whilst others must be condemned to hell; and this is implied by what He says next:

And to God belongs the first and the last [Q.LIII.25]

So both abodes[1] belong to God, and He alone acts and decides.

And God took perfect care in consoling Muḥammad (may God bless him and grant him peace) lest he be driven to despair when his people continued to treat him harshly and cruelly and refused to follow him, despite all the kindnesses he offered them, such as guidance, compassion and concern to lead them to the truth, both privately and publicly. He continued to do so despite the divine cautions which came to him, telling him not be so severely concerned with this matter. *You cannot guide (all) those whom you love, but God guides whom He wills* [Q.XXVIII.56], *It is not for the Prophet, nor for those who believe, to ask forgiveness for the idolaters, though they be near kin* [Q.IX.113], *It is the same for them whether you ask forgiveness for them, or you ask not forgiveness for them* [Q.LXIII.6], *No part of the matter is yours* [Q.III.128], and other such heart-rendering passages. Perhaps the Prophet upbraided himself for this, and felt that it was a fault on his part that the many forms of guidance he offered his people were not heeded. And so God Almighty said to him, offering consolation and encouragement:

And many an angel there is in the heavens whose intercession
avails nought save after God gives leave to whom He wills,
and is well-pleased [Q.LIII.26]

Thus, what you have experienced is not a fault on your part, nor on the part of any other intercessor; for intercession is subject to the divine Will, *save after God gives leave to whom He wills, and is well-pleased.*

1 The life of this world and the Hereafter.

That is, no creature has any influence over this matter, and no one can intercede save after the All-Merciful gives leave for intercession to whomever He wills, for whatever purpose He wills. This means that intercession is truly from God, not from anyone else: *Whoso obeys the Messenger has obeyed God; and whoso turns his back—We have not sent you to be a guardian over them* [Q.IV.80]. This means that no one has an effect on intercession but God, despite the presence of those who make the intercession. It is all in the hands of God. Yet He may decide to manifest His overwhelming grace, mercy and compassion through whomever He wills, as He did through Muḥammad (may God bless him and grant him peace), who thus stood opposed to the divine wrath in this life and [will so stand] in the hereafter. Yet in truth, it was the Real who opposed Himself, through Himself, which is exactly what the divine Names and holy Qualities necessitate, for everything is governed by this. This is why the Prophet (may God bless him and grant him peace) said, 'I seek refuge in Your pleasure from Your wrath, and I seek refuge in You from You.' This expresses the ultimate perception of the Real as both Subject and Object in every element of pleasure and wrath—yet it is too transcendent a concept for most minds to grasp. Thus, do not despair, O Prophet, that they are not able to see these things, whilst you are.

Those who do not believe in the hereafter name the angels with the names of females [Q.LIII.27]

How could such base minds hope to partake of the many forms of divine knowledge and unveiled mysteries, when they harbour such fanciful delusions, of which they cannot be rid? Even to the present day, you may find those who seek to utilise such means of drawing nigh to God, imagining that they are fortunate indeed; they argue about God without having knowledge enough to do so, and they neither listen to any counsel nor heed any caution.

They have not any knowledge thereof; they follow only surmise—and surmise avails naught against truth [Q.LIII.28]

The upshot of this is that the Veil (*ḥijāb*) prevents one from perceiving things as they truly are. All those who seek knowledge, and yet are not of those who possess true certitude (*yaqīn*) and illumination (*nūr*), have no knowledge whatsoever of the Real. They follow only surmise, and because of this their faith is sometimes strong and sometimes weak, and there is no way of knowing how it will turn out in the end. This is because they do not perceive things as they truly are, unlike those who possess true knowledge of God and who thereby recognise things at their very roots, and *enter houses through their doors* [Q.II.189]. Thus God reveals to them the realities of the Essence in which all Names and Qualities are gathered, and they know Him in the way which behoves His majesty; and their knowledge is the fruit of unveilings (*ʿayān*) and direct visions (*mukāshafa*), not proofs and arguments.[1] It is they who can truly be said to possess 'knowledge', because knowledge means to possess the object as it truly is, beyond all veils which might cover it. They are witnesses to God's Oneness just as He is a witness to this Himself, *God bears witness that there is no god but Him, as do His angels, as do those who are endowed with knowledge* [Q.III.18]. Anyone who does not reach their level cannot be said to have knowledge—at least, not any which would be recognised by those who truly know God, although he might have knowledge of God's laws. Knowledge is as noble as its object.

And if any man does not notice the mysteries and illuminations of the divine Power (*qayyimiyya*) and Sustenance (*dayyūmiyya*) which lie behind all that exists, there can be no guarantee that his heart will expel the uncertainties that lie within it in the form of doubts, delusions and surmise—for although surmise is the highest level of these uncertainties,[2] it avails naught against certitude, as the Almighty says, *and surmise avails naught against truth*.

It is curious, then, that the people who exist in this state *desire*

1 An allusion to the contrast between the gnosis of the Sufi and the rational belief of the theologian.

2 That is, to surmise something is closer to certitude than merely to imagine it, or to have doubts about it.

not to be removed from it [Q.XVIII.108],[1] despite the doubts and misgivings they suffer on its account. The cause of all this is that they have turned away from God, and have not strived to give themselves over entirely to the Holy Essence, as they should, preferring It to everything else. And since they have done the opposite, replacing the spiritual with the material, and the heart with the ego (*nafs*), they must be rejected, as the Almighty now says to His Prophet, upon whom be blessings and peace:

> *Turn, then, from him who turns away from Our remembrance, and desires only the life of this world* [Q.LIII.29]

That is, turn your entire being away from him, and do not attach your heart to the hope of bringing him out of the state he is in. '[The way] is made easy for each to become what he was created to become.'[2] *Whether you have warned them or warned them not, they do not believe* [Q.II.6]. *You warn only those who follow the Remembrance* [Q.XXXVI.11], not those who turn away from it and take their caprice as their god,[3] especially those whose hearts are completely immersed in the love of this world, and captivated by it. There is no way to guide such a person, for he is utterly annihilated and extinguished in his beloved and oblivious of all else but his goal, which is called 'the world'. The one who loves something is enslaved to it, and thus naturally he neither hears nor sees anything but it; and he looks with contempt at all those who follow any path other than his, and seek anything other than that which he seeks. We have encountered many people whose hearts have been seized by the love of this world, and we have found them to be mere images with no meaning; they do not possess *hearts with which to understand*, nor *ears with which to hear* [Q.XXII.46]; *they say 'We hear', yet they hear not* [Q.VIII.21]; *distracted are their hearts* [Q.XXI.3]. It occurred to me that they are nothing but

1 In fact, verses 107-8 of Chapter XVIII refer not to the ignorant but to the denizens of paradise.
2 A well-known *ḥadīth*: *Kullun muyassarun limā khuliqa lah.*
3 Allusion to Qur'ānic verse XXV.43.

statues, created for the purpose of reflection and admonition; *Take heed, then, you who have eyes!* [Q.LIX.2]; *They are like cattle—nay, they are further astray. They are the heedless* [Q.VII.179].

And because of the extent to which the Revelation castigates such people, it then rectifies the balance for the listener so that he does not think too badly of his fellow creatures and thus lose his sense of clemency and his cognizance of fate; therefore God says:

> *That is the extent of their knowledge. Yet your Lord knows well those who have strayed from his path, and He knows well those who are guided* [Q.LIII.30]

Thus, those who possess insight must be aware that when they view God's creatures, with all their different levels, they must do so with clemency, forgiving them for what they are. This means that we should not detach their state from the divine Wisdom, for the truth is that everything in existence is meaningful in the eyes of the divine Way (*nāmūs*). This is the point of view of the elite among those who affirm the divine Unity, one of whom said:

> Nothing is futile: men were not created vainly,
> Even if their deeds seem void of purpose;
> The Names of God are manifest in their affairs,
> The Qualities of the Essence thus made plain;
> He holds them in His two grasps, here and there:
> A grasp of blessing, and a grasp of damnation.
> It is thus; the soul may recognise it, or may not,
> Though the Criterion[1] be read to it every morning.[2]

It is as though the Almighty were saying to His Prophet (upon him be blessings and peace): *Turn, then, from him who turns away from Our remembrance*, and do not oppose him or object to his state in your heart, lest the secret of the divinely-willed fate escape you.

I say, moreover, that a man cannot realise complete resignation

1 *Al-Furqān*, a name of the Qur'ān.
2 Ibn al-Fāriḍ in his *Tā'iyya*.

(*taslīm*) to the divine Will until he discovers the true nature of predestination (*qaḍā'*) and fate (*qadar*). For otherwise, despite his best efforts, his mind will not be able to perceive guidance with the presence of error, nor purity with the presence of turbidity; and if one element of this is made clear to him, another will be beyond him. The only way he will move past this is to see how all events are enveloped by fate, and how fate itself is enveloped by the Measurer of fate.[1] When he does this, he will retain not even the slightest of doubts in the manifestations of the divine Will, and he will see everything in the best light and the most perfect way. Yet such wisdom is too precious to be clear to everyone, or understood by everyone, and only the innermost elite of those who affirm the divine Unity can hope to discover such truths—and praise be to God, Lord of the worlds!

I say, moreover, that the inner states of the spiritual elite, their secret discourse with God and their means of reaching Him and being annihilated (*fanā'*) in Him, are not easy things to speak of. Anyone who wishes to discover information about them and gain knowledge of their natures, without actually following the path they have followed, is doomed only to get further and further away from God. This still continues today; there are people who seek out information about them and argue about their intentions, as someone said:

> People say all kinds of things about us,
> Making us the target of baseless surmises.[2]

People alternate between words of praise for them [the spiritual elite] and words of condemnation, each of them basing what he says on his own reasoned opinion—yet the truth is beyond them, or we might say it never even crosses their minds. It is obvious that it occurs to no man, whoever he may be, that for the gnostic to reach God means only that he reaches his own self, nothing more; and even if he acknowledges this, he does so on the basis of faith and blind

1 The Arabic for 'fate' is *qadar*, which literally means 'measure'.
2 Ibn al-Fāriḍ in his *Lāmiyya*.

acceptance, but the true nature of it remains a mystery to him. The Scripture indicates this when it says: *Whosoever is guided is guided only to himself*[1] [Q.X.108]. That is, the furthest goal to which the spiritual wayfarer (*sā'ir*) can be guided is to be guided to his own self—to knowledge of himself, for 'He who knows himself, knows his Lord.'[2] And the furthest extent to which a spiritual wayfarer can go astray is to stray from his own self—to be ignorant of himself; thus God says, *They forgot God, so He made them forget their own selves* [Q.LIX.19].

Because of this, we say that the path which leads to God is far too hidden for even the elite to traverse, never mind the masses, despite the best efforts of the spiritual guide (*murshid*) to cast light on the way and give directions for following it; and when it comes to the understanding of the masses, the elusiveness of this path is multiplied over and again. This is why the Almighty says, *Yet your Lord knows well those who have strayed from his path, and He knows well those who are guided.*

Now it is plain to us that the 'straying' (*ḍalāl*) and the 'guidance' (*hidāya*) of which the Real speaks in this verse are not those with which the exoteric way[3] is concerned, for clearly these are not known only to God, and He has made them perfectly clear to us, *What the Messenger gives you, take; what he forbids you, leave* [Q.LIX.7]. Thus the meaning must be something deeper than that, something known only to *God and those firmly rooted in knowledge* [Q.III.7].[4] Another thing which supports what we have said is that the word *path* is ascribed to the

1 This translation reflects the Shaykh al-ʿAlawī's esoteric interpretation of the phrase, which is usually understood to mean 'Whosoever is guided is guided only for his own sake (*innamā yahtadī li-nafsih*).'
2 *Ḥadīth*.
3 Literally 'the legal way' (*al-ṭarīq al-sharʿī*).
4 The Shaykh makes it clear here that he understands this verse (Q.III.7) according to the less commonly accepted interpretation, which considers *and those firmly rooted in knowledge* to be connected to *God* by the conjunction 'and'. The more common interpretation understands that the words *and those firmly rooted in knowledge* begin a new sentence, which continues: *say, 'We believe in the book...'* See Abdullah Yusuf Ali, *The Meaning of the Holy Qur'an* (Beltsville: Amana Publications, 2004), p. 127.

divine pronoun *He*, which tells us that the path meant here is nothing other than the path of the divine Presence. Whosoever follows this path will eventually come to God; and of him who follows it not, God says, *Him We shall turn over to what he has turned to* [Q.IV.115].

And because this path is so hidden, it requires a guide, and therefore the Almighty says: *Follow the path of him who has turned unto Me* [Q.XXXI.15]. This is not like the road which leads to paradise, for it is not hidden from anyone because of how plainly manifest the way of error is, 'The lawful is clear and the unlawful is clear,'[1] except to him who is overcome by his own wretchedness, *and who takes his caprice as his god* [Q. XXV.43]; and even he is well aware that he has deviated from the straight way.

As for the way which leads to God [Himself], it is hidden from the spiritual wayfarer, whoever he is, unless he takes a companion.[2] This path is often confused with the path which leads to paradise, which the seeker might choose because he surmises it to be the best of the paths which lead to the divine Presence because of all the rewards he sees therein: *Whosoever offers a good deed shall have tenfold reward* [Q.VI.160]. So he follows this path, and when he reaches its end and the Abode of Peace[3] shows itself to him along with all it contains, he says, 'You are not what I was seeking.' It replies, 'I am your reward, and I am your appointed share.' Yet he is not content with this reward, and must be dragged into it by chains, as the *ḥadīth* says: 'Your Lord is delighted by folk who shall be dragged into paradise by chains, such that when they enter it, it grieves them.' He also said—upon whom be blessings and peace, '[Some of] the denizens of paradise moan in paradise just as the denizens of hell moan in hell,' or he said something like that.[4] The reason for this is that they have missed out on their true goal, and they would remain in this

1 Reference to a well-known *ḥadīth*.
2 Meaning a spiritual master.
3 A name for paradise.
4 *Aw kamā qāl*, 'or as he said', an expression used when the meaning of the *ḥadīth* is given, but not the exact wording.

state were it not that God will extend His goodly pleasure (*riḍwān*) to them. Thus someone said,[1] when he was shown his place in paradise as he lay dying, when he had sought something beyond that:

> If the share I have in Your love is no more
> Than what I have seen, I have wasted my days:
> Hopes in which my spirit exalted for so long,
> Yet today I see them as naught but vain dreams.
> And he continued, by saying:
> I have reached the Abode of Peace, then, it seems,
> Through the doors of my faith and my submission;
> O my Lord, then allow me to look upon You
> When I come through, and grace me with Your kindness!

The upshot of all this is that God Almighty puts His servant in the place where His servant puts Him, 'He whose emigration was for God and His Messenger, his migration was [truly] for God and His Messenger.'[2]

> *And God's is all that is in the heavens and all that it is the earth,*
> *that He might reward those who do evil with that which they have done,*
> *and reward those who do good with what is best* [Q.LIII.31]

That is, your Lord does not wrong anyone; he who follows a path will reach its end. If a man seeks the things of this world, he will not be denied them; and if he seeks the hereafter, God will reward him; and if he has no desire for either, nor for anything in the heavens or in the earth, the Real will offer Himself as his lot, and will compensate him with an aspect of His own Self, *If they are needy, God shall enrich them from His bounty* [Q.XXIV.32].

I say, moreover, that it is too often the case that a person says, 'As for those people who have such qualities, by God, their rank is so high and their achievements so great, that it is nigh on impossible to follow in their footsteps, and we must not seek anything which they

1 Ibn al-Fāriḍ in his *Mīmiyya*.
2 Reference to a well-known *ḥadīth*.

have, for we are not worthy of it;' this is what is usually said by those who are pious, never mind others. Now this is nothing other than a snare of Satan which he sets for spiritual seekers, in the hope that they might never escape it. Thus in His mercy and desire to give ease to the spiritual seekers, and in His compassion for the wayfarers, God dispels the doubts which they might have about their ability to reach Him because of their own sorry states, and tells them who exactly deserves to stand at His door, by His grace, saying:

Those who avoid heinous sins and indecencies, save lesser offences.
Surely your Lord is wide in His forgiveness. He knows you well,
when He produced you from the earth, and when you were
yet unborn in your mothers' wombs. Therefore do not
declare yourselves to be pure; He knows well
who is mindful [of Him] [Q.LIII.32]

Those who avoid heinous sins and indecencies, save lesser offences: That is, those to whom these words apply shall not be held back from their spiritual journey by the venial sins they commit. *Surely your Lord is wide in His forgiveness*, so He amends their outer forms and purifies their inner forms by means of the lights of the divine Unity which He casts therein: *Kings, when they enter a town, disorder it and make its proud folk humble; that is what they do* [Q.XXVII.34].[1] And how can the servant ever rid himself of all his faults, and thus be free to seek the Real? Ibn ʿAṭā' Allāh says in his *Ḥikam*, 'Were it that you could only reach Him after erasing all your faults and abandoning all your claims, you would never reach Him. But when He wants to bring you to Him, He cloaks your qualities with His, and your attributes with His. You reach Him by what He does for you, not what you do for Him.'[2]

1 A symbolic interpretation of this verse, wherein the 'town' represents the heart or the soul, and the 'Kings' represent God, or the 'lights of the divine Unity'.
2 Quoted in Titus Burckhardt, *The Essential Titus Burckhardt* (Bloomington: World Wisdom, 2003). See p. 272 for Moulay al-ʿArabī al-Darqāwī's commentary on this aphorism.

And because there may be, among those who seek God, some who rely on the knowledge and works they amass on their journey, and who might be turned back because of this without realising it, God Almighty wants to spare them such a fate by His grace and kindness, and says: *He knows you well, when He produced you from the earth, and when you were yet unborn in your mothers' wombs. Therefore do not declare yourselves to be pure; He knows well who is mindful* [*of Him*]. It is as though He were saying, 'Do not declare yourselves to be pure until you have been purified,' and these words are addressed—and God knows best—to those who cannot attain stability in the spiritual station of Annihilation in God (*al-fanā' fī 'Llāh*). As for the one who is completely annihilated in God, when he declares himself pure he does so by way of giving thanks to God for this blessing; thus the Prophet (upon whom blessings and peace) said, 'I am master of the sons of Adam, without any pride.' Many similar statements have been made by the gnostics; and when the gnostic says such things he is speaking with God's voice, not his own, and expressing the Essence of the Real, not his own essence; thus, he is not one of those whom this verse addresses.

And since this spiritual station is too precious to be reached by every wayfarer, and most turn back before they even begin to reach it, God in His grace wants to alert the wayfarer to this truth, lest he turn back after beginning his journey. He therefore says:

And have you seen him who turns away,
And gives a little, and then grudgingly? [Q.LIII.33-34]

The Almighty says this to strengthen the wayfarer's heart, and to warn him not to be deluded by anyone who travelled the path of guidance for a while, as God willed, and then turned back from it. He must not feel safe from God's decree, for he will only be harmed on account of his negligence towards God. It is he who is meant by God's words *and gives a little, and then grudgingly*, that is, miserly, and thus turns back from his path without realising anything. This is the only reason anyone ever turns back from God: because the self refuses to give all that it is, and the Seller is far too exalted to be outwitted by the buyer.[1] He gave good advice who said:

> Give your whole soul to the struggle against caprice,
> For if it accepts this, then what a fine effort!
> For a man who can forgo the pleasures of his soul,
> Though the whole world were offered, has truly forsaken avarice.[2]

Since this is the case, then what is gained by the one who turns back and stops following the path?

Has he knowledge of the unseen, such that he sees? [Q.LIII.35]

This rhetorical question expresses a condemnation of this person's barren intentions and his fruitless and contemptible conduct. It is as though God were saying that this person reaches nothing at all, because he does not attain any of the unseen knowledge and mysterious experiences[3] which the Folk attain.

God then reminds the one who ignorantly turns away from Him of those ancients who strove in search of the Real, that this might convince him not to turn away. He says:

Or has he not been told of what is in the scriptures of Moses,
and of Abraham, who held true? [Q.LIII.36–37]

It is obvious that had this person looked into the history of the prophets and the elite among those who affirm the divine Unity, he would not have failed in his spiritual journey. This is why the Almighty mentions here how Abraham held true to his trust; it is as though He were saying that union is born of integrity (*wafā'*), *The way of your father Abraham* (Q.XXII.78). The integrity of Abraham (peace be upon him) was shown when he gave himself up to be burned,[4] and when

1 'Metaphysical knowledge is sacred. It is the right of sacred things to demand of man all that he is.' Frithjof Schuon, *Spiritual Perspectives and Human Facts* (Perennial Books: London, 1987), p. 142.
2 Ibn al-Fāriḍ in his *Lāmiyya*.
3 *Asrār dhawqiyya*, literally 'mysteries of taste'.
4 See Q.XXXVII.83–98.

he obeyed the command to sacrifice his dear son. *Truly, Abraham was compassionate, clement* [Q.IX.114].

Al-Ḥasan[1] (may God be pleased with him) reported that Abraham never failed to hold true to anything with which God commanded him. And ʿAṭā' b. al-Sā'ib[2] related that Abraham vowed never to ask anything of a created being, and when he was cast into the fire the angel Gabriel came to him and said, 'Are you in need?' He replied, 'Not of you.'

Thus anyone who takes the least amount of time to study how the truthful (*ṣiddīqūn*) strive and how the lovers (*muḥibbūn*) long will surely see himself as remiss in his devotion to the Real, whatever be his state. Unless he gives himself to the death which for the Sufis is but a means of deliverance, *And the dead, God raises them* [Q. VI.36]. The Real should be sought above all else, for God's Presence is too dear to be purchased with affectation. For 'the Critic is discerning',[3] and however you are, so shall He be.

And since delusions afflict all kinds of seekers—for there are those of them who believe their lineage will be enough to take them along the path swiftly, and so on and so forth—God Almighty chose to dispel these delusions, lest any seeker rely on anyone else in his journey as many initiates do, relying on their fathers and their ancestors, and other things which in reality play no part in the journey to God but rather usually serve to hinder it. So He says:

> *That no soul laden bears the load of another, and that man has only that for which he strives* [Q.LIII.38–39]

This verse makes it clear to us that no man is hindered by the sin of his son, nor helped by the righteousness of his father. Therefore no man should rely on anything, in his journey to God, save that which he

1 This is al-Ḥasan al-Baṣrī, one of the *tābiʿūn*, i.e. the generation after the Companions of the Prophet, considered one of the earliest Sufis, renowned for his asceticism (d. 728).

2 One of the *tābiʿīn* and a narrator of *ḥadīth*.

3 An Arab proverb which says: 'Be devoted to your work, for the critic is discerning.' Here, the Shaykh makes God 'the critic'.

attains for himself. *We have bound each man's destiny to his neck* [Q.XVII.13], and he *has only that for which he strives*. This is the esoteric interpretation[1] of this verse, for in its most perfect sense, 'striving' (*saʿy*) only means 'seeking God', whilst to seek anything else is a waste and a delusion. I deem that it is best to understand the verse in this way, which indeed is the literal way to understand it; for if, on the other hand, we took 'striving' to mean 'seeking reward', this would require further interpretation, since a man can benefit from the prayers of another, as is the case with intercession, and there are clearly other ways in which he can derive benefit from the deeds of others. Yet this verse states that this cannot be, and therefore it must refer to the journey to God; for the wayfarer cannot benefit from the journey of anyone else, but only when he himself is sincere can he reach his goal. Thus the *ḥadīth* states, 'When My servant comes a hand's span nigh unto Me, I go an arm's length nigh unto him; and when he comes to Me walking, I go to him at speed.' This is what God means by saying:

And that his striving shall surely be seen [Q.LIII.40]

That is, he shall immediately attain to the fruits of his striving, unlike the one who seeks the hereafter and thus does not attain to his desire until he dies. And though death may be near, the Real is yet nearer, *We are nearer to him than his jugular vein* [Q.L.16]. The distance is only long for the one who turns back, and *gives a little, and then grudgingly*, as was said before. Were they only to be sincere to God, it would be better for them. Someone[2] said, condemning those who are thus described:

Though they offer only vain hopes, they decry what fate offers them;
They plunge into the sea of love, yet are not wetted;
They seek to travel without getting up from their places;
They tire themselves out in their journey, yet get nowhere.

This is the state of one who does not hold true to his pledge. As for the one who pledges to God that he will never look to anything

1 *Al-fahm al-khāṣṣ*, literally 'the special understanding'.
2 Ibn al-Fāriḍ in his *Lāmiyya*.

other than Him, and holds true to what he pledges to God, *Unto them the Most Merciful shall give love* [Q.XIX.96].

Then he shall be rewarded with the fullest reward [Q.LIII.41]

That is, more than he can imagine. Someone[1] said:

> I attained my desire, more than I ever hoped for,
> O! What rapture, were this to stay evermore with me!

What God has in store for the righteous is greater than anything. And since the perfect soul will accept nothing other than the Real as the reward of its efforts, it always worries lest its destiny be anything other than to look upon Him, and thus it naturally yearns always to hear a reassurance from God which will increase its peaceful certitude that its goal will not be marred in any way. So the Almighty answers this soul in a way which befits the divine grace, saying:

And that unto your Lord is the uttermost end [Q.LIII.42]

This gives peace and assurance to hearts that they have attained the good pleasure of their Beloved; *And in this let them rejoice; it is better than all that they amass* [Q.X.58]. This is the most which the servant can ask from his Lord, and it is what they call 'annihilation in God' (*al-fanā' fī 'Llāh*). For to find one's uttermost end with Him means necessarily to be annihilated in Him, since contingent beings cannot coexist with the Timeless Being (*qidam*), *And when your Lord revealed Himself to the mountain, He made it crumble to dust* (Q.VII.143). Thereupon He subsists, and there is no creature: 'I am his hearing wherewith he hears, and his sight wherewith he sees...' Then there is revealed to the servant the reality of existence, which is that nothing exists but God, and there is nothing to be seen besides Him. *Do you testify that besides God there are other gods? Say: I do not testify. Say: He is but One God* [Q.VI.19]. He is speaking of all this when He says:

And that it is He who makes to laugh, and makes to weep;

1 Ibn al-Fāriḍ in his *Lāmiyya*.

And that it is He who makes to die, and makes to live;
And that He Himself creates the two kinds, male and female,
Of a drop when it is cast forth;
And that upon Him rests the second genesis;
And that it is He who gives wealth and contentment;
And that it is He who is the Lord of Sirius[1] [Q.LIII.43–49]

And that it is He who is He, to the infinite reaches of 'He-ness' (*Huwiyya*), in the manifestation of 'I-ness' (*Anāya*): *He is the First, and the Last, the Manifest and the Hidden* [Q.LVII.3]. This is as far as any seeker may reach; and here are opened for him the dominions of heaven and earth, and he sees nothing in addition to the One and Only: *God is the light of the heavens and the earth* [Q.XXIV.35]. Thus it is no surprise that he should say, *This is my Lord!*[2] [Q.VI.76], *The way of your father Abraham* [Q.XXII.78], *And he was not of the idolaters* [Q.II.135]. For when *he saw a star, he said 'This is my Lord,'* and he only said this after he had witnessed [the Truth]. And do not be grieved by their claim that Abraham did not have knowledge of divine matters at that time,[3] for *this is but the words they speak with their mouths* [Q.IX.30], and *They have not any knowledge thereof; they follow only surmise*. Someone who has no knowledge of the divine nature might say, 'What does your Lord do with things, that they become imperceptible to the gnostic when he is in the throes of annihilation?' The answer is, *Say: My Lord scatters them as dust, and leaves them a level plain, wherein you can see neither crookedness nor curve* [Q.XX.105–107].[4] So do not deem what we have said far-fetched, for He is well able to do it.

1 Sirius is a star that was worshipped by the pagan Arabs.
2 As Abraham did when he beheld the star, the moon and the sun.
3 Some of the theologians say that when Abraham underwent this experience, he knew nothing about God and was not a prophet, and this is the only reason he mistook the star for his Lord. See for example Muhammad Asad, *The Message of the Qur'ān* (Gibraltar: Dar al-Andalus, 1984), p. 184.
4 These verses are usually interpreted to refer to the events of the Last Day and thus translated in the future tense, but the Shaykh al-ʿAlawī interprets them here to signify how all created things are rendered non-existent for the one who is annihilated in God.

And that He destroyed ʿĀd, the ancient,
And Thamūd, and did not spare them,
And the folk of Noah before—truly, they were yet more evil and more insolent; And the Subverted City He did overthrow,
So that there covered it that which covered [Q.LIII.50–54]

That is, He destroyed and overthrew them all into a deep abyss; and this is just what He does with all creation in the eyes of the gnostic when He shows His magnificence to him, for He does not allow it to mix with anything else. This is signified by His words *so that there covered it that which covered*; that is, all created beings are covered and enveloped by the resplendent lights of direct witnessing (*anwār al-shuhūd*), so that they cannot be seen on their own, but only seen through the manifestation of the Almighty within them.

And since man usually deems it far-fetched that the Almighty could be manifested in all that is grand and all that is lowly, and in all that is great and all that is small; and since he thus belittles the works of his Lord, the Almighty says to him:

Which, then, of your Lord's boons do you dispute? [Q.LIII.55]

That is, which of God's boons do you belittle, disputing that it could be worthy of the divine manifestation? The truth is that all things are enveloped in the divine Quality which engendered them, and *the heavens are enfolded in His right hand* [Q.XXXIX.67], and all things draw their being from His Names and Qualities. Someone[1] said:

When you deem any ugly thing to be His Deed,
The beauty in it comes rushing towards you.

And since the Almighty has just spoken comprehensively of things which nevertheless cannot be grasped by most ordinary people, He now alerts us of this fact, so that His words are not mistaken for simple platitudes:

1 Ibn al-Fāriḍ in his *ʿAyniyya*.

This is a warner, of the warners of old! [Q.LIII.56]

That is, of those secrets which were vouchsafed to the first of the prophets and messengers, and which the Real in His glory chose to reveal to the people of the latter days, as an honour to His prophet Muḥammad (may God bless him and grant him peace) that the people of knowledge among his community might share in what was granted the prophets of the Israelites,[1] 'The sages are the heirs of the prophets.'

Yet since hearts are so difficult to unite[2] and so reluctant to receive counsel, even when it comes to the precious truths and subtle mysteries we have just expounded, the Almighty warns them by saying:

The Imminent is imminent;
Apart from God no one can disclose it.
Do you then marvel at this discourse,
And do you laugh, and not weep,
Haughtily turning away? [Q.LIII.57–61]

So strange it is, then, that you find it so difficult to acknowledge the truth of this imminent reality, laughing in scorn and derision at him who speaks of it, though his Lord has given him insight into it. And you do not weep for what you have lost from God, although you are yourselves lost, and have squandered your lives aimlessly. Someone[3] said:

For his own self let him weep whose life is lost,
Without his gaining anything from it.

And you haughtily turn away, oblivious to all the indications and signs which come to you and are presented to you.

Whatever be the case,

Bow yourselves before God, and worship. [Q.LIII.62]

That is, even if you have lost out on the deepest knowledge of Him,

1 Allusion to a *ḥadīth*.
2 That is, to have one purpose, to concentrate on one thing.
3 Ibn al-Fāriḍ in his *Mīmiyya*.

this does not mean that you are remiss in worshipping Him; for there are those who are meant to serve Him and earn His paradise, and there are others who are meant to love Him and earn His presence. He says: *Each We succour, these and these, from your Lord's bounty; and your Lord's bounty is not confined* [Q.XVII.20].

Closing Prayer

Lord, You who give in abundance, I ask you with my heart and my tongue to grace us with Your largesse, and treat us with Your kindness, and not to veil us by what we are from what You are. Lord, You who give each soul what it earns, do not entrust us to our own selves, and do not make our fortunes veil us from our responsibilities; unless our fortune be purely from You, Lord, in which case make it an ample fortune. Lift from us the veil which covers us, and hold us lightly in your Hand and draw us towards You, and increase our delight and our joy. And send blessings upon our liege Muḥammad, and increase his greatness and his light, for I cannot bless him as he should be blessed, but I leave his blessing to You. And be well pleased, Lord, with all who have followed him from our time to his, and have mercy on all those who walked in their footsteps, and strove to make him victorious. And send peace upon him, peace which radiates to all those who cleave to the truth and keep mindful of it.

These lines were completed, as God allowed it, and to the satisfaction of him who wrote them, on the morning of Sunday, the fifteenth of Dhū'l-Qiʿda, 1333 AH. May God increase us all with light upon light.

The Key to Mystical Knowledge in the Commentary on the Chapter 'Time'[1]

Praise be to God, who marked His saints with the gnostic teachings (*maʿārif*) He makes flow from their tongues, and the subtle mysteries He bequeaths them. May blessings and peace be upon the noblest of His prophets and the dearest of His saints, our liege Muḥammad, and upon his Family and Companions, and upon all his community, the first and the last of them. Amen!

Ibn ʿAlīwa,[2] the servant of his Lord (may God strengthen his deed and magnify his reward) says: One of the noble scholars (may God cause the clouds of mercy to rain upon his grave) asked me to speak a little about *Sūrat al-ʿAṣr* according to the way of special understanding (*al-fahm al-khāṣṣ*).[3] Since he had such trust in us, we fulfilled his request by producing these few sentences; for how could we possibly say all that there is to be said about such a vast ocean? All that we ever wrote on the subject amounted to no more than a few pages, which were printed in Tunis by one of our friends who has an interest in spiritual realities and esoteric teachings. Now since all our copies of it have run out, and there are those who still desire to have it,

1 *Miftāḥ ʿulūm al-sirr fī tafsīr sūrat al-ʿaṣr*, Mostaghanem, n.d.

2 One of the Shaykh's forebears, al-Ḥājj ʿAlī, was known locally as ʿAlīwa, a colloquial diminutive, which led to the name Ibn ʿAlīwa being given to his descendants, later becoming al-ʿAlāwī and finally al-ʿAlawī. The Shaykh referred to himself by all three names in his writings and poetry. The publishing house in Mostaghanem which is dedicated to publishing the Shaykh's works uses one of the forms of the Shaykh's name: al-Maṭbaʿa al-ʿAlāwiyya.

3 The word *khāṣṣ* is translated here 'special', but it also has the meaning of 'select' or 'of the elect'. *Khāṣṣ* is the opposite of *ʿām* which can be translated as 'general' or 'common'.

and disciples who long to read it, we have renewed resolve to see it reprinted, with the addition of a few more brief sentences, which we hope will benefit the disciple. If what I say therein is correct, then it is from God; and if I err, I will not be the first to err, and God knows I do not do so intentionally. Here, then, for the disciples, is some of what I understand on the subject.

The Almighty says, after *In the Name of God, the Compassionate, the Merciful*:

> *By Time,*[1] *verily mankind is in ruinous loss* [Q.CIII.1–2]

This is an oath sworn by God to emphasise man's ruinous loss, in addition to the emphasis imparted by the word 'verily.' That He uses this emphatic language implies that man is unaware of his loss, and that he is unlikely to perceive it as long as he does not sense the truth of what his state was before his spirit entered his physical body. Had he imagined this when he was still a pure essence, free of all corporeality and hence decay, he would have acknowledged what a loss it would be compared to the state he was in. Yet how can he perceive this now that he is a prisoner of his lusts, locked in the cell of his nature? This state puts him as far as can be from the attainment of his eternal felicity; and thus will he remain as long as his inner eye (*baṣīra*) does not penetrate the wall of his prison and see what lies beyond it, and this cannot happen without a clear proof, *You cannot pass without authority* [Q.LV.33].[2] Thereupon, he will perceive his ruinous loss when compared to the state he was in before his spirit entered his body; were he able simply to imagine it, this emphatic language would not have been required.

Now as for the word *ʿaṣr*, the exegetes have interpreted it in many

1 The word *ʿaṣr* can mean 'afternoon', 'era' or 'time'. Although in the context of this Qur'ānic Chapter it is usually rendered 'afternoon', the Shaykh al-ʿAlawī focuses his commentary on the meaning 'time', in particular its divine connotations, hence our rendering of it as 'Time' here.

2 'Without authority', i.e., without the permission or will of God.

ways, the most fitting of which is that it means 'time', as was the opinion of Ibn ᶜAbbās (may God be pleased with him). The reason He swears by it is because it is the most strange of all created beings. One aspect of its strangeness is illustrated in the words of the Prophet (may God bless him and grant him peace) as narrated by Ṭabarānī on the authority of Abū Umāma with a sound chain, 'Do not revile Time, for Time is God.' Another version has it 'Do not revile the moment, for the moment is Time, and Time is God.'

Despite the above tradition, we usually define time as being determined by the motions of the heavenly bodies; this would mean that it is borne of a contingent being, and all that is borne of a contingent being is itself a priori contingent. Yet if we give a moment's reflection to the aforementioned tradition, it will force us to discard this definition for an altogether different understanding of time than that which we have previously imagined, and it will cast us out into an endless ocean, and our rational cogitations will *come away dazzled and defeated* [Q.LXVII.4]. Or else, we will see that 'Time' here does not mean the time we know, composed of the material motions of day and night. In any case, the time known to us is not bereft of its share of the rays of this ever-flowing Presence without beginning or end; that is, whose beginninglessness and endlessness are each without end. With respect to this beginningless and endless flow, does the thing we know as 'time' simply disappear in that Substance of Pure Being, or does it have a certain independence? If we consider the latter, then the mind would find it impossible to conceive of anything like it among created things, in that its past and its future do not exist, and its present is a part of it which cannot be divided; it is in fact the fate (*qadar*) that separates what is past and what is future. Thus it is almost too subtle for the imagination to touch upon. This pertains to the position of man within it; and from this point of view, man can barely even acknowledge its existence.

On the other hand, if we conceive of time with respect to its progression through the seasons, or its division into days, months and years, and we consider it to be governed by comings and goings, and increase and decrease, this ascribes corporeality to it and moves it from the realm of imagination to that of sensorial affirmation, and the soul is then able to acknowledge it. From this perspective, the mind does not hesitate in affirming its existence, nor its contingency or its being a container for contingent things, nor its being subject to change, variation and vicissitude. Because of all the thoughts and assumptions this might lead to, the Lawgiver issued a prohibition against all who might seek to disparage it, saying, 'Do not revile Time, for Time is God.'

In sum, strangeness is an inseparable part of time whether this be in its name, its reality or its vicissitudes. Say what you will about it, it is inherently inscrutable. Another aspect of its strangeness is that the Prophet (may God bless him and grant him peace) would sometimes swear by it. It is related from ʿĀ'isha (may God be pleased with her) that he would sometimes recite it thus, *By Time, and by its vicissitudes*. I do not say that this was a canonical reading, though; for he may well have said it by way of exegesis.

Let us now return to an examination of the literal meaning of the verse. The definite article *alif-lām* prefixed to the word *insān*, 'man', implies that these words refer to the whole species: 'mankind'. This means that the entire human species is judged to be in ruinous loss, save for those who are thereafter exempted. This is a true pronouncement from God Almighty, even though mankind are unaware of the nature of this loss, which is why the sentence contains these emphatic elements[1] such as the word 'verily' and the oath, which is the highest level of emphasis. All this implies that the human being is not aware of his own loss, and yet his mind is not free of preoccupations either; for otherwise, all this emphatic language would not be necessary. The verse also implies that man is in a state of the utmost loss precisely *because* he does not sense it, beguiled as he is by his own evil

1 The author here lists the Arabic forms of emphasis in the verses, some of which are not translatable into English.

deeds, and ruled as he is by his own passions, as God affirms, *Thus have We made each nations deeds beguiling for them* [Q.VI.108].

As for the nature of the loss, it is nigh impossible for man to picture it as long as he remains in his present state, until he compares what he has lost with the state he is presently in; that is, unless he compares his physical life with what his spiritual life was before the spirit entered the body, when the spirit roamed freely among the Supreme Assembly[1] and swan in the ocean of lights, as far as could be from the taint of all that is other than God.

The soul then was in a position of great nobility and privilege, receiving its call directly from God without any intermediary, and giving an unambiguous reply.[2] It retained a share of this nobility even after its Fall and its attachment to the first human body; for He crowned it with the crown of knowledge and adorned it with the jewels of understanding, teaching it that which it had not known before.[3] Sufficient proof of this is that He made the angels prostrate before it, and before every human soul in the seeds of the loins of Adam. Yet when it [the soul] was enclosed in the body, it gained an outer form which it had not had before; this made man imagine that he was but another kind of animal, acting according to the nature of his species.

How vast, then, is the gulf between the two levels, and the distance between the two states—that of the First Man, and that of the second man—because of the blinding light between the two levels. The difference is so great that they are almost two different beings, and it would not be far-fetched for us to say that the First Man is not the second man. The word 'man', then, has two meanings: one is this human being we consider a kind of animal, who can be seen and touched in the flesh, distinguished only by his species; the

1 Of angels and beatified spirits.

2 This is an allusion to Q.VII.172: *Remember when your Lord took the seeds of the sons of Adam from their loins and made them bear witness against themselves, and said: 'Am I not your Lord?' They said: 'Yea, we testify.'*

3 This refers to the creation of Adam. See for example, Qur'ānic verses II.30-34.

other has attributes and distinctions which make him virtually the opposite of the first. The first is called the 'tangible (*maḥsūs*) man', the second the 'transported (*manqūl*) man'. Or we might say that the first is called the 'animal (*ḥayawānī*) man', the second the 'lordly (*rabbānī*) man'; and one should strive not to be animal but to be lordly. God says, *Nay, be lordly; for you have taught the Book, and you have studied it constantly* [Q.III.79].

When is a lordly man? It is when he voyages from his outer being to his inner being, and shakes off the burden of his own ego (*nafs*), that he may behold his own nobility and glory, from which he has until then been veiled. There he will find riches and a magnificent kingdom; and when he comes to know the primordial state of the human soul, as it was in the realm of perfection, he will say, 'I have been given a kingdom greater than was ever given to any being!' That is eternal felicity; and it was to this that Imām ʿAlī alluded when he said, 'You were created for eternity.' This is the man of inscrutable nature, known for his elevated status: he is the man *created in the most perfect rectitude* [Q.XCV.4]; and the other is the man *reduced to the lowest of the low* [Q.XCV.5]. The former is the object of God's words *We created you…* [Q.VII.11], and the latter of His words *…and then We formed you* [Q.VII.11]; thus the First Man is created, but not formed. It is to this that the *ḥadīth* alludes, 'God created Adam in His form;' he did not say 'God formed Adam in His form,' because the creation came before the form, and that which was created in His form had no form of its own. Thus there is no form at all: neither for the First Man, nor for that which was created in the First Man's form. You can see, then, that man has lost as much knowledge about himself as he has about his Lord, because he has forgotten what he used to be, *They forgot God, so He made them forget themselves* [Q.LIX.19].

In sum, the ruinous loss of man is that he thinks it is his body that makes him human. He has the ability to come to realise the glory he has lost, but only if he can see that it is his spirit that makes him human. The reason the verse says he is *in* this loss—that is, that this loss contains him—is to imply that this loss surrounds him and all of his kind, save only for those whom the following verse exempts:

Except they that believe and do good works, and exhort one another unto truth, and exhort one another unto patience [Q.CIII.3]

How few they are, who are endowed with these great and noble qualities that earn for them happiness untainted by the least grief, neither in the short nor the long term; for one might believe but not do good works; and one might do good works but not exhort unto truth; and one might exhort unto truth but not unto patience. Ultimate salvation, however, cannot be attained or even imagined in its fullest sense without the combination of these four qualities, namely faith (īmān), good works (*al-aʿmāl al-ṣāliḥa*), the enjoining of truth (*al-tawāṣī bi'l-ḥaqq*), and the enjoining of patience (*al-tawāṣī bi'l-ṣabr*) for the sake of truth.

If a person should miss out on his share of faith in the life of this world (God forbid), he will *suffer a manifest loss* [Q.IV.119], which will make him say, when he sees the joy of the saved and the grief of the damned, *O, would that I were but dust!* [Q.LXXVIII.40].

If he does attain to his share of faith in this life, so that he is separated from the realm of unbelief in God and His Messenger, he thereby takes a large step in the direction of his salvation and eternal bliss; but his feet are only made firm by means of good works. 'Good works' is a class containing every praiseworthy act, and excluding every blameworthy act. This takes him another step closer to salvation and bliss; but his feet will not yet be totally firm unless he moves on to exhortation unto truth. The person who does not exhort unto truth will likely not remain on the way of truth, since the chief of all good works is to enjoin what is right and condemn what is wrong. If one neither enjoins what is right nor condemns what is wrong, there is a risk that one day he will neither adhere to what is right nor abstain from what is wrong.

Now since these qualities (speaking the truth, adhering to the truth and exhorting unto truth) usually require one to endure things he dislikes, God links them to exhortation unto patience. If one does not fortify himself with patience, he is unlikely to remain firm in the call to God Almighty. Luqmān's[1] advice to his son puts us in mind of this; the Holy Qur'ān tells us that he said, *Enjoin what is right, and condemn what is wrong, and bear with patience all that afflicts you. Indeed, that is of the steadfast heart of things* [Q.XXXI.17]; that is, it is a quality of those who are steadfast of heart.

In sum, part of exhorting unto truth is enjoining what is right and condemning what is wrong, as we have said; and part of exhorting unto patience is bearing harm as well as preventing harm. These noble qualities are found in the prophets (upon whom be blessings and peace) naturally, and in all other guides (may God be pleased with them) by a certain amount of effort, although this effort is eased by the prophetic inheritance, 'The sages are the heirs of the prophets.' This is what the prophets (upon whom be blessings and peace) have bequeathed, and it is what the sages have inherited from them. Those who have knowledge should reflect on their share in this bequest, and on their sincerity and the level of devotion to God, His Messenger and the believers. If they find something in their characters to indicate that they indeed have a share of this bequest, then let them hold on to it. If not, this means that their connection has been severed, and they must look for someone to re-establish it for them before they breathe their last breath and leave this world in such a state, and thus bitterly regret the circumstances of their deaths. For after this life there is only Paradise or Hell; may God save us, and all who submit to Him, from a bad end.

Man's foremost duty, then, is to strive for his soul's salvation by doing all he can to meet God Almighty with a clear conscience; and the believer's conscience can only be completely clear if he loves for

1 Luqmān is the subject of *Sūrat Luqmān*, Chapter XXXI of the Qur'ān. He was a wise figure of old, known to the pre-Islamic Arabs; in the Chapter, he gives a series of advice to his son.

his brother what he loves for himself.[1] This above all is what gives the spiritual guide the incentive to give others sincere guidance towards God. He wishes for salvation and eternal triumph for himself; how then can he be at ease, and how can his heart be tranquil, when he sees his fellow man, and the people of his faith, in the state that they are in, when he loves for them what he loves for himself? In this, he follows the noble *ḥadīth* which states that the believer is not truly a believer until he loves for his brother what he loves for himself.

All in all, the struggle of this sort of person is perpetual, and it is something upon which perfect faith is contingent, as we have mentioned above. May God make me, and you, among those who believe, do good works, exhort unto truth, and exhort unto patience.

1 Reference to the well-known *ḥadīth*, 'None of you [truly] believes until he loves for his brother what he loves for himself.'

The Outspreading Tree of Mysteries On the Meaning of the Invocation of Blessings on the Chosen Prophet[1]

In the Name of God, the Compassionate, the Merciful

The great teacher, renowned for the transmission of the Supreme Name, out liege Abū'l-ʿAbbās Shaykh Sīdī Aḥmad b. Muṣṭafā al-ʿAlawī al-Mustaghānimī (may God favour us and the Muslims by giving him His good pleasure, and preserving his memory) was asked to speak about the invocation of blessings upon the Prophet (may God bless him and grant him peace) and explain its sublime meanings. He answered with the following:

Lord God, I praise You with all my heart as well as my tongue, O You who draw the sincere to ever higher ranks of spiritual virtue! You grant Your grace to whomsoever You will, and you are the source of all grace, honour and favour. I bear witness that You are the One, the Only, the exclusive Possessor of being (*wujūd*) and engendering (*ījād*); and I bear witness that our master and liege Muḥammad is Your Messenger, he who was completely prepared to receive Your perfect theophanies (*tajalliyāt*). Bless him, Lord, with all Your generosity; send upon him blessings and peace commensurate with the purpose You gave him, and send them too upon his Family and Companions, who gave succour to the truth and carried its banner. Have mercy, Lord, on the goodness that remains in this Community, and rain down upon their bodies, spirits and hearts from the clouds of mercy.

1 *Dawḥat al-asrār fī maʿnā al-ṣalāt ʿalā al-nabī al-mukhtār*. Mostaghanem: al-Maṭbaʿa al-ʿAlāwiyya, 1991.

Aid them, bolster them and strengthen them with every proof, argument and wisdom. Amen!

First of all I would like to address he who was the direct cause for this book's being written, our righteous and sincere friend in God, Sīdī Muḥammad b. al-Ḥabīb b. Mawlānā al-Ṣiddīq.[1] May God make each of us one of those who fulfil the covenant they made with Him!

Sīdī, after first seeking the blessing of your mention, and asking after you, and wishing you perfect peace in every way, as you deserve, I say: I was honoured by your letter; and after reading it with the utmost reverence it seemed to me that it was nothing short of a message from one of profound wisdom and knowledge. I set my eyes upon it and concentrated my thought on it, and found it to be a verdant meadow and a blossoming flower, enough to prove the worth of its author. I say this especially of the part concerning the prophetic vision (upon its source be the best of blessings and greetings).[2] It is naught but a blessing for which you must give thanks—and I praise God that such people as you remain in existence! As for the request you have made of us to explain the contents of the invocation of blessing [on the Prophet] which God caused to flow from your lips, we do not have anything more to offer (and God knows best) than what you yourself have. Yet in obedience and service to you, and in hope of partaking in the grace of blessings upon the Prophet (may God bless him and grant him peace), I say, acknowledging my own shortcomings:

The meaning of the invocation of blessings (*ṣalāt*) differs according to its subject and its object. With respect to the subject, if it is God, then of course it does not mean the same invocation which is required of His creatures, since from Him it is *act* (*fiʿl*), while from others it is *speech* (*qawl*): a kind of prayer, which has been explained

1 The Grand-Shaykh of the Ḥabībī branch of the Darqāwī Ṭarīqa (d. 1972).

2 As the Shaykh al-ʿAlawī mentions above, this treatise is in response to a letter sent him by Shaykh Muḥammad b. al-Ḥabīb who had had a vision of the Prophet in which the Prophet gave him a form of invocation of blessings (*ṣalāt ʿalā al-nabī*). For the original Arabic text of this *ṣalāt ʿalā al-nabī* see Appendix II.

as 'a request for mercy accompanied by an attitude of reverence,' and other similar interpretations, as we shall see. In any case, it is a prayer.

Now if it is from God, it differs according to the identity of the object. It is clear that the blessings He sends upon all believers are not the same as the blessings He sends upon the elite among them, *They are the messengers; We favoured some of them over others* [Q.II.253]. If [as this verse shows] there is a hierarchy of favour among the elite, then there must certainly be one among the masses. There are those whom He blesses by taking them out of the darkness of idolatry and into the light of faith (*nūr al-īmān*); there are those whom He blesses by taking them out of the light of faith and into the mystery of certitude (*sirr al-ayqān*); and there are those whom He blesses by taking them out of the mystery of certitude and into direct vision (*wuqūᶜ al-ᶜiyān*); and there are those whom He blesses by taking them out of direct vision and into the effacement of all identities (*faqd al-aᶜyān*); at this point, the Subject of the blessings overwhelms the object, 'I am his hearing, his sight...'[1]

I say, moreover, that God has made the act of blessing His prophets and His chosen ones the opposite of cursing His enemies, since cursing means exile, rejection, cutting-off and veiling. God's blessing is an expression of His love and affection, His nearness and manifestation, and His appearance to the object of the blessing according to his aptitude. In the case of the masses of ordinary believers, what they receive from God is His affection for them in the form of whatever mercies they merit; and in the case of the elite, what they receive from God is nothing other than Him, for they will not be satisfied with anything less, *Faces that day shall be resplendent, looking upon their Lord* [Q.LXXV.22-23].

There is also a hierarchy among the elite, determined by the extent of the theophanies shown to them. The Real draws near to some and grants them knowledge of Him through His Deeds. Others are granted knowledge of Him through His Names, others

1 Sacred *ḥadīth*.

are granted knowledge of Him through His Qualities, and still others are granted knowledge of Him in His Essence; this is the 'greatest sign' of which He speaks when He says, *He saw, of all the signs of his Lord, the greatest* [Q.LIII.18].

Were they correct in saying that the blessing of the Prophet meant only mercy, he [the Prophet] would have attained to this when God said, *We sent you only as a mercy to the worlds* [Q.XXI.107], which means that he became mercy itself. Yet the truth is that he continued to desire and seek what lay beyond that; he said (may God bless him and grant him peace), 'In prayer has been made the joy of my soul,' and said, 'The truest word any poet every said was: "Lo, all save God is naught."' That is, all things, whether they be worldly or otherworldly, are nothing in the eyes of prophethood, unless they are channels for the beholding of the perfections of the Essence, and the lights of the Qualities. And since the trustee of this particular formula of invocation of blessing[1] knew well the wishes of the Prophet (may God bless him and grant him peace), and that he never sought anything but his vision of the Beauty of the Essence, no matter how many other kinds of mercies came to him, he asked God to bless Muḥammad as he truly merits, saying:

> Lord God, with all the forms of Your perfections, in all of Your manifestations, bless and grant peace to our lord and master Muḥammad, the first of the lights which emanate from the ocean of Your Essence's magnificence; he who realises, in the realms of the inward and the outward, the meanings of Your Names and Qualities. He is the first to give praise and to worship with every form of devotion and offering; and it is from him that everything in the realms of spirit and form derives. Blessings too be upon his Family and Companions—a blessing to lift for us the veil from his holy face, both in visions and the waking state, and acquaint us with

1 Meaning Shaykh Muḥammad b. al-Ḥabīb, the author of the letter to the Shaykh al-ʿAlawī.

> You and with him in every rank and presence. By his eminence, Lord, be kind to us in all movement and all stillness, in every look and every thought. *Glory be to your Lord, the Lord of power, above all that they ascribe to Him; and peace be upon the messengers; and praise be to God, Lord of the worlds!* [Q.XXXVII.180–182].[1]

He [Shaykh Muḥammad al-Ḥabīb] is saying, as it were: Lord God, you know exactly what Your Prophet wants from You, and that he desires nothing but the vision of Your Beauty; so show him love, draw him nigh, and acquaint him with You, and show Yourself to him in all the perfections of Your Essence (*al-kamālāt al-dhātiyya*), as they exist in all Your active (or we might say 'physical and spiritual') manifestations. Give him this always, and comfort him, and make him secure (*amminhu*) when these theophanies descend upon him, that he may attain not only what he wishes from You but what You wish from him. This is the kindness and protection that everyone who reaches God sorely needs, and it is what is called 'peace' (*salām*) in the language of the Law; *Their greeting therein shall be peace!* [Q.X.10], which here refers to the denizens of Paradise alone. For every one who is in possession of a favour (*niʿma*) asks nothing from God but its preservation (*salāma*).[2] This is why it is said that the invocation of blessings (*ṣalāt*) must be accompanied by the invocation of peace (*salām*), so that there is equilibrium (*taʿādul*) and the favour of God to the object of the invocation can be made complete. Blessing alone, though it is a favour from God, has no guarantee of permanence unless it is accompanied by peace from Him. Because of this, no matter how noble blessing is, peace will always be nobler—but only

1 This prayer came to be known as the 'Treasury of Truths' (*Kanz al-ḥaqā'iq*), and forms part of the daily litany of Ḥabībī disciples.

2 *Salāma*, which is here translated as 'preservation', is also 'safety' and derives from the same root as 'peace' (*salām*). In all that he says here, the Shaykh al-ʿAlawī is returning to the necessity for equilibrium or stabilisation after the descent of the divine theophanies. *Amān*, *salāma* are contained in the invocation of peace (*salām*), which is the total expression of the divine 'safeguarding'.

when it is preceded by blessing; it is not equal to it when they are taken separately, since blessing means for God to approach the servant as he merits, whilst peace means for this approach to be secured, and is therefore judged according to what precedes it.

Now because God's blessing is assured for Muḥammad (may God bless him and grant him peace) by His words *Verily, God and His angels send blessings upon the Prophet* [Q.XXXIII.56], the following commandment from God that blessings be invoked on Muḥammad is not given any further emphasis; that is, He does not say 'Invoke abundant blessings upon him' as He says *And give him abundant greetings of peace* [Q.XXXIII.56]. It is as though He were saying, 'My approach and manifestation to Muḥammad is assuredly abundant, so make plentiful requests that he be granted stability (*thabāt*), and safely kept in the state he is in.' To ask for stability and safety for him is to ask it for his community; and God knows best what He means.

If it be asked: Why have some scholars said that it is allowed to invoke peace on non-prophets, yet not blessings?

We say: We have seen that the meaning of blessing makes it too precious to be freely invoked on just anyone, save for the prophets and angels, except in the case of lists.[1] As for peace, its purpose is to request safety for the person with regard to his inner state with God. Thus it can be freely invoked on any believer, who will receive it according to his rank. Thus to request it for non-prophets is not to request the impossible; and this is why it has been allowed by some.

I say, moreover, that the prophets (upon whom be God's blessing and peace) have been singled out for the simultaneous reception of blessings and peace from God, unlike the saints. In the case of the latter, blessing from God might come to one of them and yet the peace might be affected by an obstacle, a delay or by an interval. This is why the saints, unlike the prophets, sometimes display things

1 That is, if non-prophets follow prophets in a list of names, it is permitted to invoke blessings on them, as in: 'May God bless Muḥammad and his Family and Companions.'

that seem unnatural and possibly contrary to the Sacred Law, simply because the saint does not have the necessary protection from God for that spiritual station, which has been bequeathed incompletely. As for those who are firm in the station after having inherited it,[1] almost invariably they display nothing at all which seems contrary to the Sacred Law or to nature (and by 'nature,' we mean that nature which is truly sound, not merely the nature of the masses). This is because the spiritual station has been bequeathed fully.

So when the constant bond of blessing and peace upon the Prophet is maintained, the grace is passed along to its inheritors in the right way. These two divine gifts which the Sacred Law calls 'blessing' and 'peace' are identical to what the Sufis call 'intoxication' (*sukr*) and 'sobriety' (*ṣaḥw*), or 'annihilation' (*fanā'*) and 'subsistence' (*baqā'*), or other expressions they have for them; and in truth, these things cannot be expressed in words.

Now since the aspiration (*himma*)[2] of the spiritual elite is higher than a desire for contingent beings, it always revolves around the axis of the divine Names and Qualities and seeks out the perfections of the Essence which lie beyond this. God provides for man according to his aspiration; and when the aspiration is great, it only asks for what is greater still. The Prophet (may God bless him and grant him peace) said, 'When you ask of God, make the request great'; and there is no nobler request or greater aspiration than an aspiration which turns away from creation and attaches itself to the True King. Thus the request of the saints (may God be well pleased with them) is restricted to their goal; both for themselves, and for others.

As for the words 'with all the forms of Your perfections': [*anwāᶜ*] is the plural of *nawᶜ* 'form', and it is unlimited when ascribed to the Divine, because His perfections (*kamālāt*) are infinite. Thus the author

1 That is, inherited from a prophet; a reference to the *ḥadīth* mentioned above: 'The sages are the heirs of the prophets.'
2 *Himma*, meaning spiritual aspiration or resolve, is an important concept in Sufism. It refers both to the disciple's resolve and concentration on the path and also to the master's radiation of his own spiritual power to the disciple.

of the prayer asks God to show Himself to Muḥammad (may God bless him and grant his peace) with every one of His perfections, so that with every perfection that is revealed, another follows which is even more perfect. Nabahānī says in his *Hamziyya*:

> You continue to rise up over every 'over,'
> Ascending: an ascent which has no end.

And so on, unto infinity, *The last shall be better for you than the first* [Q.XCIII.4].[1]

The theophanies (*tajalliyāt*) conform to the perfections,[2] being equally infinite, *Were you to count God's favour, you would never number it* (Q.XVI.18). This is true if they are manifestations of the divine Acts, and all the more true if they are manifestations of the Essence and the Qualities, *God is the Infinitely-Vast, the All-Knowing* [Q.II.115].

Know, moreover, that the way of the gnostics has always been to pass on their knowledge through the prayers of blessing they compose for the Prophet (may God bless him and grant him peace), so that this can be a means of ascent for those who follow them, guiding them to certain mysteries of the Divine and secrets of prophethood. This is why the author of this prayer calls Muḥammad (may God bless him and grant him peace) 'the first of the lights which emanate from the ocean of the Essence's magnificence.' We can glean from this that he was the first light from which the springs of Manifestation poured forth. He himself said (may God bless him and grant him peace), 'The first thing God Almighty created was my light.' From this light all other lights were kindled, and all other levels of being derive.

Now 'light' means that which allows one to see, whether one is speaking of the physical or the intellectual; the former refers to the revealing of outward things, and the latter refers to the revealing of

1 We have translated *ākhira* in this verse as 'the last' in conformity with what the Shaykh al-ʿAlawī wishes to express here. The usual translation is: *The latter will be better for you than the former* or *The hereafter is better for you than this world.*

2 The Shaykh al-ʿAlawī is here referring to the part of the prayer: 'in all of Your manifestations'.

mysteries; the former is an aid for the eyesight, and the latter an aid for the insight. The things which are easiest to understand are those which are illuminated by outward appearances, even though in reality they are only branches of those things which are hidden away in the obscurity of the mysteries. Thus, however diverse the roots and widespread the branches, they all have their source in the One Light, *God is the Light of the heavens and the earth* [Q.XXIV.35]; this is the Pure (*mujarrad*) Light.

As for the subsidiary (*iḍāfī*) light known as Muḥammad (may God bless him and give him peace), He compares it by saying, *The symbol of His light is as a niche* [Q.XXIV.35]. *His light* is Muḥammad (may God bless him and give him peace); this is why the simile here falls on the subsidiary, not the Owner of the light, which in reality is the First Light.[1] Thus God's transcendence (*tanzīh*) is preserved, and not compromised by being made the subject of a comparison (*tashbīh*)—although in fact His transcendence is identical with His immanence,[2] *wheresoever you turn, there is the Face of God* [Q.II.115]; each perspective must nonetheless be given its due. Were the Pure Light the subject of the simile, there would have been no need to add the pronoun 'His,' and He would have said simply 'the Light is as a lamp,'[3] since there is symmetry between the lamp and the Light. It would also have implied that the inward reality is limited by the outward manifestation, and that the niche and the *glass*[4] were other than the light; yet in fact, they are *light upon light* [Q.XXIV.35], which implies that the subject and the object of the comparison are united in the light; and *all things come unto God* [Q.XLII.53]. This makes it clear to us that God is a Light which is pure of materiality and relativity—that is, *there is nothing like unto Him* [Q.XLII.11]—and that His revealed light, which is called Muḥammad (may God bless him and give him peace) and which is subsidiary to the Pure Light, is *like a niche wherein is a lamp* of God's mystery, and is

1 That is, the verse says 'The symbol of His light', not 'the symbol of Him' or 'the symbol of the light'.
2 *Tashbīh* means both 'comparison' and 'immanence'.
3 Rather than *the symbol of His light is as a niche wherein is a lamp*.
4 The verse continues: *the lamp is in a glass*.

necessary for His sustaining power to pervade in every substance and accident, *God is the Light of the heavens and the earth*. The lamp has the greatest share of God's Light: *Whoso obeys the Messenger has obeyed God* [Q.IV.80].

In sum, God alludes to that part of the Muḥammadan Light which is material with the word 'niche,' and alludes to that part of it which is subtle with the word 'lamp'. The lamp is the light of the glass and the niche, and *God is the Light of the heavens and the earth*. A tradition states that 'God Almighty created all creation in darkness, and then sprinkled His light onto them.' That is, He decreed their creation in His pre-eternal knowledge, and then lent something of His Being to them. In any case, we have been drawn into examination of a verse[1] which is not our present subject; God willing, we shall give a full commentary of it elsewhere.

The point to be made here is that everything that pours forth from the Mostly Holy Emanation (*al-fayḍ al-aqdass*), in all its varied spiritual and material manifestations, has as its foundation the Muḥammadan Light, from which all other lights were kindled, including the heavens and the earth. We should not find it far-fetched that the hard, corporeal things we see around us are actually rays of the Holy Presence (*ḥaḍrat al-quds*); for if they are perceived otherwise, that is a result of weakness of insight. When the defect is removed from the one who beholds these effects, he no longer sees them at all, and comes to behold their origin, which is light upon light; and *look once more: can you see any fissures?* [Q.LXVII.3]. Indeed not! One finds nothing but inner reality and outward manifestation, and that outward manifestation is what is called 'light'; whosoever is guided to it has truly been guided. *God guides to His light whom He will* [Q.XXIV.35]. The Prophet (may God bless him and grant him peace) was asked, 'Do you see your Lord?' He answered, 'I see Him as light.'

This light is what prevents the innermost Essence (*al-kunhiyya*) from being seen; God's veil is His very manifestation, and because of

1 Meaning the Verse of Light (Q.XXIV.35).

its brilliance He is concealed. The tradition says, 'His veil is light.' The manifestation of the subsidiary light [i.e. the Prophet] veils the Pure Light; light can only be seen in light, and the inner reality can only be seen in the outward manifestation. The Prophet (may God bless him and give him peace) said, 'Whosoever sees me has seen the Real'; that is, whosoever knows me knows the Real. By 'sees me', he does not mean the being called Muḥammad bin ʿAbdullāh; rather, he is alluding to his true reality which pours forth from the ocean of the Essence's magnificence, for this is the locus of His manifestation. God said: 'My earth and My heaven encompass Me not; but the heart of My believing servant does encompass me.'[1] This is the heart which is manifested in all hearts, and the spirit which is manifested in all spirits, and the soul which is manifested in all souls: *Your creation and your upraising are but as a single soul* [Q.XXXI.28]. Whoever comes to know this soul, and sees the spiritual in the material, will not be denied his share of the rays of the Holy Presence; and this is only realised in a precious few individuals, due to the aptitude God places in them, in addition to the attribute of perception which all human beings share. These precious few are the prophets and the innermost elite of the saints. Thus the author of this prayer praises the station of prophethood by calling the Prophet (may God bless him and grant him peace) 'he who realises, in the realms of the inward and the outward, the meanings of the Names and Qualities.' By this reckoning, he is the only one to have realised this completely; all others have done so only relatively, by means of spiritual inheritance, 'The sages are the heirs of the prophets.'

We say 'he is the only one to have realised this completely' because he was the first locus of the Essence's manifestation—or we might say: he was the first to whom the Names and Qualities became attached—therefore his inner state (*bāṭin*) was equal to his outer state (*ẓāhir*), and his beginning (*awwaliyya*) equal to his end (*ākhiriyya*);[2] and because of this,

1 Sacred *ḥadīth*.

2 An allusion to the divine Names the Outer (*al-Ẓāhir*), the Inner (*al-Bāṭin*), the First (*al-Awwal*) and the Last (*al-Ākhir*).

he was the greatest intermediary between the Real and His creation. Thus he said (may God bless him and give him peace), 'I was a prophet when Adam was between water and clay,' though he was not physically sent until much later, and thus he brings together the beginning and the end, to which he alluded when he said, 'We are the last, who came first.' With this, the beginning is joined to the end; and a thing may end with itself, the branch reaching down to the root. This is God's way with His creation, *Verily He who has made binding upon you the Qur'ān will bring you home once more* [Q.XXVIII.85]. And the Prophet (may God bless him and grant him peace) said, alluding to the meaning of this, 'Time has been cyclical since the day God created the heavens and the earth.' The generality of the allusion makes it clear to us that prophethood is a circle like a ring, composed of individual points, namely the prophets; and the dot which connects the two ends of the ring's circle is Muḥammad (may God bless him and grant him peace). And because of the special status he has in that his point was chosen, from all the other points, to complete the circle of prophethood, he said, 'I am the master of the sons of Adam, and [I say so] without pride.'

Moreover, when we reflect on the circle of the ring of prophethood[1] after its two ends are brought together, it becomes clear to us that every single point of it connects its two sides, such that if you were to remove it the connection would be broken. From this perspective, all the points are equal, which is why he said (may God bless him and give him peace), 'Say not that I am better than my brother Jonah.' *We make no distinction between any of His messengers* [Q.II.285], because distinction would be a defect in the circle of prophethood.

We have seen that this circle is a single whole composed of interconnecting points, and that its end is identical with its beginning. Its reality is the Supreme Spirit (*al-rūḥ al-aʿẓam*) which conveys messages

1 In Arabic, 'the ring of prophethood' and 'the Seal of Prophethood' are both expressed by *khātam al-nubuwwa*. *Khātam* means both 'seal' and 'ring'. The term *khātam al-nubuwwa* is very familiar to Muslims as term for Muḥammad, the final prophet. The Shaykh al-ʿAlawī intentionally uses the term here, taking advantage of the dual meaning of *khātam* in order to make a play on circularity and finality.

from God, and it is none other than the Muḥammadan Breath (*al-nafas al-Muḥammadī*) and the Eternal Spirit (*al-rūḥ al-abadī*) which was breathed into Adam who was the first point on the circle. Someone said, speaking with the tongue of the Aḥmadian[1] Reality:

> Though I appear to be the son of Adam,
> There is in me a part that makes me his father.

Because of this, prophethood in reality is Muḥammad's (may God bless him and grant him peace), in whichever of the points of the circle it manifests, because (as we have seen) it is a single entity, even though it is named by many names. Whoever looks upon the circle after all its points have been connected will say, *We make no distinction between any of His messengers* [Q.II.285]; and whoever looks at it before that, or whose aspiration does not discern what is there, will say, *We believe in part, and disbelieve in part* [Q.IV.150]; and the part cannot contain the meaning of the whole. All we have just said allows us to arrive at the meaning of 'Seal of Prophethood' (*khātam al-nubuwwa*), which applies to him (may God bless him and grant him peace) in two ways: firstly, as we have just seen, he is the point which brings together the two sides of the circle of the ring,; and secondly, he is the ring itself.

The above affirms that prophethood is one, and that he [the Prophet Muḥammad] is its reality, which means that he is the Seal of Prophethood in every way. It has also been said that the reality of prophethood is the Supreme Spirit which conveys messages from God, and not the specific body which can be seen by everyone. It was to this that Uways al-Qarnī (may God be pleased with him) alluded when he said, 'You all know no more of Muḥammad (may God bless him and grant him peace) than one who knows only the scabbard of the sword.' He was alluding to the Supreme Spirit, which comes down to reside in that body, just as God's Eternal Speech came down to reside in the Holy Qur'ān: the body is a signpost of the spirit-reality, just as the book is a signpost of the Eternal Quality.

1 Aḥmad being a name of the Prophet.

Now since he was chosen to receive God's messages from the beginning of the Holy Emanation, his noble spirit was that which made the covenant on behalf of all other spirits on the day of *Am I not your Lord?* [Q.VII.172], because it is the intermediary for everything that is conveyed [from God]; otherwise, what would be the meaning of the primacy of his prophethood? It is to this that the author of the invocation alludes when he says, 'He is the first to give praise and to worship with every form of devotion and offering.' He is the first to give praise through the totality of his light (*nūrihi al-kuliyy*), and the first to give worship with every form of devotion and offering through his individual parts (*juz'iyyātih*).[1] Nabahānī (God be pleased with him) said:

> Your light is the whole, and mankind are parts,
> O prophet under whose banner the prophets march!

The Almighty says, *All things did we gather in a indisputable imam*[2] [Q.XXXVI.12]; and no imam has a plainer or truer right to imamate than him. The general allusion for the gnostics here is that all things are gathered and combined in his reality, but the mind is quick to deny this without even reflecting on what is there. However, when God takes one by the hand and shows one the branch in the root, one will find that every single thing is contained in the Muḥammadan Reality, with a containment that is total. From this point of view, he is indeed the worshipper who worships 'with every form of devotion and offering.' It is easy to have faith in this, but it is difficult to understand it when one witnesses the many ways that individuals oppose [the Divine] in the world. Yet after one uses one's intellect and insight, it may become clear to you that *There is nothing that does not sing His praises* [Q.XVII.44]. Though opposition (*mukhālafa*) subsists, it is as nothing in the eyes of the Almighty Knower: *None know the hosts of your Lord*

1 Reference to the ring of prophethood as a whole and the individual parts of the ring.

2 In this verse, the word *imam* is usually interpreted to mean 'book' or 'record'; the Shaykh al-ʿAlawī here takes it at its face value: 'leader'.

save He [Q.LXXIV.31]; for what may appear to be opposition from the point of view of divine approbation (*riḍā*) is in accordance with the divine will (*irāda*). *And had your Lord willed, they would not have done so* [Q.VI.112]. Indeed we are spared the need for further clarification by the Almighty's words, *He said to it, and to the earth, 'Come forward, willingly or unwillingly!' The two said: 'We shall come willingly'* [Q.XLI.11]. Once true vision (*shuhūd*) is attained, we recognise that everything that once seemed ugly to us is not ugly in its true substance:

> When you deem any ugly thing to be His Deed,
> The beauty in it comes rushing towards you.[1]

A suitable example of this occurs to me: behold how the Holy Qur'ān combines things that are divergent. It contains mention of higher realities and lower ones, of obedience and disobedience, of divine lore and pharaonic lore, and so on beyond count. *We left nothing out of the Book* [Q.VI.38]. It is diverse from the point of view of its dependents (*mutaʿalliqāt*), and unified in its reality. We worship God by reciting what it contains of the accounts of false doctrines, just as we worship by reciting what it contains of the accounts of the divine Essence and Qualities. Every word of it, no matter what it attaches to, *cannot be touched save by the purified* [Q.LVI.79]. This is so because it is ascribed to the Word of God; and if you were to divorce it from this ascription, it might not be permitted to mention it. Thus, he who looks at the universe as it is in reality will see it as nothing but a niche wherein is a lamp—if, that is, he sees the niche from the front. If, however, he sees the niche from the back, he will see nothing but darkness, because it is not open at both ends,[2] *In the inside of it there is mercy, while against the outside of it there is torment* [Q.LVII.13].

1 Ibn al-Fāriḍ in his *ʿAyniyya*.

2 That is, if a niche contains a bright lamp, but you look at the niche from behind the wall, you will not see the light that fills it. What the Shaykh al-ʿAlawī is saying is that if one is ignorant or blind to the holiness of the universe, it might appear to be monstrous or meaningless, because one is beholding it from the wrong perspective.

The sun in its brilliance is not diminished
If the blind man cannot see it.

The author's words 'and it is from him that everything in the realms of spirit and form derives' exclude only the realm of the Eternal (*ʿālam al-qidam*); all else is drawn from him, just as the branch is drawn from the root.

Concerning his words 'Blessings too be upon his Family and Companions,' the meaning of family and companionship is not beyond the reach of general understanding. As for its inner meaning: the true possessors of the family connection are those who have a connection to the Muḥammadan wellspring; that is, those who are near to him, and are thereby part of the Family no matter who they are. 'Salmān is one of us, one of the Household.' Nābulsī (may God be pleased with him) said:

O, what a bond that was given to Salmān,
By the word of Ṭāhā,[1] the Messenger of God, the finest prophet,
'Salmān is one of us,' one of the Household,
Though he was a Persian, and not an Arab!

This is the true inherited lineage in the eyes of the Folk. As for companionship, it includes all those who accompanied him in the same station, such as his fellow prophets and the innermost elite of the saints, although within this station there is a hierarchy, *They are the messengers; We favoured some of them over others* [Q.II.253]. All those who fall outside this group [of 'family' and 'companions'] are not included in this invocation of blessing, according to our interpretation of it. As for how the masses understand the term, it includes—in addition to his household and descendants (may God be pleased with them)—every believer.

His words 'an invocation of blessing to lift for us the veil from his holy face, both in visions and the waking state' mean: may He make it [the invocation of blessing] for us a means to lift the veil from his

1 Ṭāhā is one of the name of the Prophet.

true unique reality, as has just been described. The author (may God be pleased with him) then felt concern, and feared that this vision would bar him from what is more important than it, namely the synthesis of the two visions, and steadfastness in the two presences; and so he said: 'and acquaint us with You and with him in every rank and presence.' He is saying, as it were, 'I ask you, our Lord, to acquaint us with him in a way that does not veil us from our acquaintance with You; and grant us a view of him which does not bar us from a view of You, so that we can fulfil both requirements in every rank and presence.' This is the most precious thing to which one can aspire, for it is the upright way and the straight path requested by His words *Guide us upon the straight path* [Q.I.6]; and it is the most precious thing in existence, and the most difficult to behold, because it is the position of equilibrium between two extremes,[1] and is thus like an attempt to combine opposites; and each one proceeds in accordance with his inner reality: *God has not made for any man two hearts in his breast* [Q.XXXIII.4]. But God's aid makes even the most difficult of things easy.

And since this path is so subtle and narrow, and the one who traverses it so fearful and anxious, as the Prophet (may God bless him and grant him peace) said, 'I am the nearest of you to God, and the one of you who fears Him the most;' for the nearer one gets, the more one fears ruin—because of this, the author says, and I say with him, 'By his eminence, Lord, be kind to us in all movement and all stillness, in every look and every thought.'

Glory be to your Lord, the Lord of power, above all that they ascribe to Him;
And peace be upon the messengers;
And praise be to God, Lord of the worlds!

1 That is, between the created and the Uncreated.

Appendix I

The Shaykh al-ᶜAlawī's Answers to Questions on Qur'ān and Ḥadīth: Selections from *The Freshest Spring: Answers and Letters*

Questions and Answers on the Subject of the Qur'ān

I

QUESTION: Following a discussion amongst his followers about the meaning of God's remembrance of us, the Shaykh was asked about the verse *Remember Me; I will remember you* [Q.II.152].

ANSWER: As for our remembrance of Him, it is that we say *Allāh, Allāh*, or any of the other Most Beautiful Names of God. This is obvious, and presents no difficulty. Now as for His remembrance of the one who remembers him, it is somewhat difficult to envisage its mode and form. How could such a thing be? [The Shaykh said this to inspire his followers to give an answer; but when he saw that the matter was beyond their ken, he said:][1] With this noble verse, the Almighty is drawing our attention to the thing that can immortalise us in history. It is as though He were saying, 'If you wish to be remembered with respect by future nations and generations, then remember Me, and I will remember you on their tongues.' Because of this, you see that those who remember God remain known to the masses and the elites; in this way, God remembers them—an apt reward, since acts are rewarded like for like. God knows best.

1 This is a gloss by the anonymous editor of the collection.

2

QUESTION: How may we reconcile God's words to the Prophet (may God bless him and grant him peace) *Indeed, you guide towards a straight path* [Q.XLII.52], and His words *It is not for you to guide them, but God guides whom He will?* [Q.II.272].

ANSWER: Guidance (*hidāya*) is of two kinds. The first kind is general, and in His grace the Almighty bestows it upon every single human being; it includes the intelligence, by which one distinguishes between what is harmful and what is beneficial, and also includes the sending of prophets to show people the right path. It is to this guidance that God refers when He says, *Indeed, you guide towards a straight path*. This means that the Prophet (may God bless him and grant him peace) leads people to a fork in the road, one fork leading to salvation and the other to damnation, and explains to them where each path leads. This form of guidance is the work of the prophetic envoys, and it is of this guidance that He speaks when He says, *As for Thamūd, We guided them, yet they preferred blindness to guidance* [Q.XLI.17]. That is, they chose the path of damnation instead of that of salvation.

As for the second kind of guidance, it is the grace of success (*tawfīq*) in following the path of salvation, which is given by none but God Almighty, *My success can only come from God* [Q.XI.88]; that is, it is not something that anyone can acquire by his own power. It is of this that God speaks when He says, *It is not for you to guide them* [Q.II.272], *You guide not whom you love* [Q.XXVIII.56], and other passages to the same effect.

3

QUESTION: The Shaykh was asked about the words of Abraham (upon whom be peace) in the Qur'ān: *'Lord, show me how you give life to the dead.' He said, 'Have you not faith?' He said, 'Yes, but* [*show me*] *so that my heart may be at rest.' He said, 'Take four birds, and tame them to you, then set a part of them on every hill, then summon them, and they will come to you with speed'* [Q.II.260]. The questioner said, 'This verse implies to us that our master Abraham's heart was not at rest concerning the existence of the Resurrection (*al-nash'a*); yet such a thing is impossible for a prophet.'

ANSWER: Our master Abraham (upon whom be peace) meant, by his question, to attach the last stage of his faith (*īmān*) to the first stage of his witnessing (*shuhūd*). This is the way it is done on the Path of God, and thus we could rightly say that this was a lesson from Abraham to us, so that we do not suffice ourselves with the faith we have when it is within our means to fasten it to a certain amount of direct witnessing (*mushāhada*); for the faith of one who believes based on second-hand accounts and proofs is never as strong as that of the one who experiences direct witnessing. This is equally true of the words of our master Moses (upon whom be peace), *Lord, let me look upon You!* [Q.VII.143]. The upshot of this is that the heart is only truly set at rest with doctrines when they are supported by a certain amount of direct witnessing; and God knows best.

4

QUESTION: The Shaykh was asked about God's words *You are the best people ever brought forth [as an example] for mankind; you enjoin good and condemn evil...* [Q.III.110].

ANSWER: These words address either the believers in general, or the elite among them. If they address the believers in general, they would mean that they [the believers in general] have been singled out among all people for the task of enjoining good and condemning evil, because this is the task of the truthful, the prophets and the messengers. It would also mean that their enjoining and condemning would be addressed to other peoples; and 'evil' would mean idolatry and its concomitants, and 'good' would mean the doctrine of divine Oneness and its concomitants. On the other hand, if these words were addressed to the elite among the believers, it would mean that the enjoining and condemning would be addressed to the believers themselves; 'evil' would mean every blameworthy trait, and 'good' would mean every virtue.

Personally, we consider the latter explanation to be the correct one, since the words in their fullest meaning can only apply to the guides of mankind who call to the Real by the way of truth, of whom the Prophet (may God bless him and grant him peace) said: 'The earth will never be bereft of forty men with hearts like the heart of the Friend of the Merciful.[1] By means of them are you given rain, and by means of them are you given provision. Every time one of them dies, God replaces him with another.' Likewise, for every other prophet there are those among the community of Muḥammad (may God bless him and grant him peace) with hearts like their hearts. It is to these people, who are present in every age and every land, that these words are truly addressed, because they are worthy of this and were primordially destined for it. The propensity to enjoin good and condemn evil is natural to them, not cultivated in them; it may also exist in others, but only extrinsically.[2] I believe that this class of people usually exists only among the invokers, 'they who neglect all for the invocation of God', as a *ḥadīth* says. Now the one who neglects all for the invocation of God (or who is infatuated with the invocation of God, as another narration has it) is only to be found among the Sufis; no one else reaches their level of invocation, whoever he may be, unless he is one of those who loves them, or is one of their predecessors, or is one of the people of their spiritual lineage—may God protect us from speaking ill of them!

5

QUESTION: The Shaykh was asked about how to reconcile God's words, *And if a good thing is visited upon them, they say, 'This is from*

1 That is, Abraham. See footnote 1 page 56.
2 That is, others acquire this trait from outside rather than it being innate in them.

God'; but if an evil thing is visited upon them, they say, 'This is from you.' Say: 'Everything is from God' [Q.IV.78], and what He says shortly after this, *Whatever good is visited upon you, it is of God; whatever evil is visited upon you is of yourself* [Q.IV.79].

ANSWER: All systems of divine Law revolve around a single axis, which is to gather people's hearts to the One True Agent, who is the only one active within existence, and in whose hand is all good and evil. This was the main reason for ending the messengers (may blessings and peace be upon them all), because the peoples of the world attributed—and indeed still continue to attribute—most actions to beings other than God Almighty, which contradicts the doctrine of pure divine Oneness. One aspect of this is that they would attribute good fortune and bad fortune to their prophets, even though the purpose of the prophets was to direct them to God, as we can see here in God's words to the Prophet Muḥammad (may God bless him and grant him peace), *Say: 'Everything is from God.'*

It is a curious thing to mistake the object of an action for its subject. This is why the divine words express incredulity, *How is it with this people? They scarcely understand any tiding* [Q.IV.78]. The only reason they were in this condition is that they ascribed actions to people other than their true Agent.

Now once this verse had made it clear that God is the only agent, the soul desired to cling to this principle and abandon any other perspective. God therefore strengthened it with the next verse, commanding it to keep to this position, and never to ascribe any action to anything but God—and if it cannot avoid doing so, then at least to ascribe what is bad to itself and no one else, and to see this as a result of its own poor choice.

The second verse also seems to affirm the existence of acquisition;[1]

1 Acquisition (*kasb*) is the term used by the Ashʿarī school of theology to reconcile free will and predestination: God 'creates' the action, and the human being 'acquires' it by choice.

this is why the Sacred Laws were ordained and the messengers sent. It may be that the 'evil' of the second verse is not identical to the 'evil' of the first: the first may refer to the misfortunes that befall one in his possessions and physical person, whilst the second may refer to sin. Now it is vile indeed to attribute sin to God, since this would make a dead letter of the Sacred Laws. However, the same is not true of ascribing the misfortunes that befall one's possessions and physical person to God, since this is only the result of the doctrine of pure divine Oneness.

In sum, it is not right to attribute natural disasters of any kind to anything but God. But when it comes to the sins that a person commits, it is not appropriate to attribute them to anyone but himself, since the evil deed is his choice; he took it up and accepted all that it entailed.

Now if you ask why we do not attribute his good deeds to him, too, since they are also his choice, and he takes them and accepts all that it entails, I say that indeed this is the case; the difference is that God legislated good deeds, whilst the servant is the one who legislates his evil deeds, by his own will.

6

QUESTION: The Shaykh was asked about God's words *But for the grace of God and His mercy upon you, you would all have followed Satan, save a few* [Q.IV.83]. This verse seems to suggest that some would not have followed Satan even if they had no grace or mercy from God. How can this be?

ANSWER: The exoteric understanding of this verse is that God was addressing certain specific people with it, and reminding them of how He blessed them by sending the Prophet (may God bless him and grant him peace) and revealing the Book. He is saying to them, 'but for the grace of God, the Book, and His mercy which is the Messenger, you would have followed Satan.' That is, you would have remained idolaters, save a few—namely those who attained to faith by using their intellects, before the Book was revealed.

Now as for the esoteric understanding, it is that all guidance that comes to man, of any kind, is the result of God's grace and mercy; were it not for that, no one would be guided—save for those whose innermost reality refused to stray from the path of guidance, such as Muḥammad (may God bless him and grant him peace) who is by his very nature a manifestation of mercy, and opposed to falsehood. All things conform to their innermost reality. According to this understanding, the exception refers to him and his fellow prophets and messengers, and the meaning is, *But for the grace of God and His mercy upon you, you would all have followed Satan*, save for those who are the embodiments of mercy such as Muḥammad and his fellow messengers, upon all of whom be blessings and peace.

7

QUESTION: The Shaykh was asked about God's words, *This day have I perfected for you your religion* [Q.V.3].

ANSWER: I see that I am forced to make mention of something which is often returned to in your writings,[1] and in the writings of other contemporary authors, and something you have mentioned in your latest book, too, by way of attacking the new practices[2] of the Sufis and asserting that they are foreign to Islam. Your greatest support in this is God's words *This day have I perfected for you your religion, and fulfilled my favour upon you, and has been My good pleasure to choose Islam for you as your religion* [Q.V.3]. By this, you mean to suggest that anything which was not part of the religion at that time could never be part of the religion thereafter.

1 It seems the question was posed by a reformist scholar opposed to Sufism.
2 Opponents of Sufism charge that Sufis are guilty of committing heretical innovation (*bidʿa*) because of those practices of theirs which were not performed by the early Muslims. The Shaykh uses the word *muḥdathāt* here for 'new practises', rather than *bidaʿ* 'heretical innovations'.

Now this is all very well as a way of rejecting all the new practices of the Sufis such as prescribed invocations (*waẓā'if*) and the like; but it cannot be accepted unless we follow it to its logical conclusion and reject, alongside them, all the legal opinions of the jurists and statements of the scholars. This would mean doing away with all the religious laws deduced by means of scholarly reasoning, and judging them as alien to the religion, because they only appeared after the religion had been perfected and God's favour to the Muslims had been fulfilled, as the verse clearly states. Thus this assertion of yours would lead us into beliefs that have never been espoused by any heretical Muslim sect, let alone by the orthodox followers of the *Sunna*, to whom you belong. For the jurists declared things lawful, unlawful, obligatory and recommended, and innovated more laws than can be listed; and they did all this after the religion was perfected and the favour fulfilled.

So what will the respected Shaykh say to all this? Will he gladly assert that from the beginning of the age of juridical reasoning until this day the Muslims have been worshipping God with something other than the religion which was revealed to the Prophet (may God bless him and grant him peace) and which was sealed by God's words *This day have I perfected for you your religion*? And it does not stop there, for all this equally applies to the laws derived from the statements of the Companions and the Second Generation, and even the recorded acts of the Four Righteous Caliphs, since all of this was after that holy verse was revealed. Surely you are not unaware, respected Shaykh, of the situations that arose for the first time in the era of the Caliphs? Have you not heard that the act of praying the *tarāwīḥ* prayer[1] in the mosques in congregation was not established until the rule of ʿUmar, and at his order? This was not the practice during the lifetime of the Prophet (may God bless him and grant him peace). And the simultaneous triple pronouncement of divorce was counted as only one pronouncement at the time of the Prophet (may God bless him and grant him peace), during the rule of Abū Bakr, and during part of the

1 A special evening prayer offered in Ramaḍān.

rule of ʿUmar (may God be pleased with them both), until the latter began to consider it as three pronouncements; and the Companions all agreed, and this remains the way it is viewed to this very day. Take also the legal penalty for public drunkenness: at the time of the Prophet (may God bless him and grant him peace) and Abū Bakr, it was forty lashes, but ʿUmar raised it to eighty and it remained that way. The same can be said of many other situations that arose. The fact is that all these things occurred after this holy verse was revealed—are you happy, then, to say that all this is alien to the religion? Of course you would never say such a thing, nor would any other Muslim.

I believe you are aware that the matter does not stop there, either; for it must apply also to all the rulings derived from those prophetic *ḥadīth*s which came after this verse was revealed—that is, after the religion was perfected and the favour fulfilled—since they are no different to anything else, as far as the literal import of the verse goes. Now if we take the view that all the *ḥadīth*s that came after that verse may not be used as evidence, we would make a dead letter of all the *ḥadīth*s for which we have no certain date—and this is true of more than a few *ḥadīth*s—lest we worship God with a religion other than that completed religion of which He said *This day have I perfected for you your religion*. After all, the narrators of *ḥadīth* usually did not give anything to indicate the date. Now there is no doubt that to assert such a thing would cause a calamity for us and for all Muslims, as you must know.

Now I have an inkling that you believe that the matter would stop there, but I fear I must tell you that in fact it would be even graver still; for to take this doctrine to its logical conclusion would mean rejecting several divine rulings that are ordained by Qur'ānic verses, and declaring that they are alien to the religion. Let me clarify this for you in a way that should give you pause, even if only for a moment, until finally you will see the truth and logical conclusions of it. Suyūṭī says in his book *al-Itqān*:

> One difficult passage is God's words *This day have I perfected for you your religion* which were revealed at

> ʿArafāt in the year of the Farewell Pilgrimage, and seem to be saying that all the obligations and laws of Islam had been perfected at the time it was revealed. Several people have affirmed this, even though it is related that verses pertaining to usury, debt and certain details of inheritance were only revealed at a later date. Ibn Jarīr was also confused by this, and said, 'The best interpretation of it is that it means their religion had been perfected by their having established it in the Sacred City, and the idolaters having been banished.'

The reason this is relevant here is that it would mean we would have to remove the laws based on these [later] verses from the religion; and by God, it is utterly inconceivable that any Muslim could believe such a thing. This is why the exegetes have interpreted this verse in many ways, none of which resemble the interpretation advanced by the authors of our times.

It is my opinion that the best interpretation of this verse is that the 'perfection of the religion' means the perfection of its foundations and essential principles. As for the things which branch off from this, we do not think that they are included here—and nor do you, respected Shaykh—except in the sense that the branches are derived from the roots, and are considered to be contained within them, just as the tree is contained within the seed. May God inspire me, and you, with knowledge whose foundation is reverence of God (*taqwā*).

This is what we understand to be the meaning here of 'religion' and its 'perfection', and the 'fulfilling of the favour' upon those who follow it. If this is acceptable to you, then so be it; if you have another view, then please guide us to a better understanding than this, may God reward you for it!

Be sure, respected Shaykh, that your understanding of this holy verse is baseless, and should not be believed. I do not say that you actually believe this in the sense that you explicitly stated it after much reflection and scrutiny, or that you based it on proof and evidence; rather, I think that you stated it without fully thinking it through, and that you were aided in this by your own self-confidence because of your scholarly credentials. Yet the truth is that both we and you are people of whom it can rightly be said that we know some things and are ignorant of others; and the best thing for the likes of us to do, before anything else, is to recognise our own shortcomings even in what we *do* know, never mind in what we know not.

So the obligation of sincere advice requires us to say to you what was said in *al-Risāla al-Khurūbiyya*:[1]

> The jurist should be kind to himself, and recognise his place in the religion, and not stretch out his empty hand to the gnostic stations and lordly states which are beyond his reach—until he has first tasted what the true men have tasted.

May God not deprive us, or you, from the wellsprings of their mystical knowledge.

Lastly I implore you, sir, not to use the sacred texts as evidence of your views until you have reflected on them thoroughly, for this is no laughing matter. This is the advice I have already chosen to give myself, and I choose the same for you. Peace.

8

QUESTION: The Shaykh was asked about God's words *Their sight overtakes Him not, but He overtakes their sight* [Q.VI.103], and if this means that it is impossible to see the Almighty.

ANSWER: I do not see anything here to suggest that it is impossible to see the Almighty. The verse speaks of 'overtaking' (*idrāk*), not 'seeing' (*ru'ya*), and overtaking is not the same as seeing. Overtaking means to perceive a thing exactly as it is in every way, which is impossible in the case of the Almighty, and cannot be done even by the inner sight of the heart, never mind the eyesight.

1 A work of the Algerian jurist and Sufi Muḥammad ibn ʿAlī al-Khurūbī (d. 1556).

I say, moreover, that if seeing God were impossible, whether according to reason or revelation, Moses (upon whom be peace) would not have asked it of God, because he knew better than anyone what is possible and impossible with respect to Him. Even if we acknowledge that the vision was denied him, it is entirely possible that it was reserved for someone else, *These are the messengers: We favoured some of them over others* [Q.II.253].

9

QUESTION: The Shaykh was asked about God's words …*Thereafter, when He gave them a righteous son, they assigned Him associates in what He had given them* [Q.VII.190].[1] Why is Adam (upon whom be peace) described in this way?

ANSWER: If ever sin, idolatry or the like are attributed to Adam, it refers to the progeny he sired, with all their various doctrines. He was like a ship, carrying them all. This is true of every prophet who sired children, save for those who had no idolatrous progeny such as Muḥammad, John and Jesus (may God bless them and grant them peace); for nothing has been related which appears to attribute sin to them.

10

QUESTION: The Shaykh was asked to comment on God's words *He who is guided is guided only for himself; and he who errs, errs only against it* [Q.X.108].

ANSWER: On the plane of esoteric understanding, the first thing that comes to mind when hearing this verse is that guidance is determined by self-knowledge, and error is determined by self-ignorance. The

1 The preceding verse says: *It is He who created you out of one living soul, and made of him his spouse that he might rest in her. Then, when he covered her, she bore a light burden and passed by with it; but when it became heavy they cried to God their Lord, 'If You give us a righteous son, we indeed shall be of the thankful'* (Q.VII.189).

Almighty is saying, as it were, 'Whoso is guided in such a way that he shall never err thereafter…' This is why the guidance is restricted by the word *only*: in other words, whoso is guided is guided to nothing other than his own self,[1] that is, to knowledge of it as it really is. This is suggested by the well-known tradition, 'He who knows himself, knows his Lord', and vice versa: he who is ignorant of himself is ignorant of his Lord, which is represented here by His words *and he who errs, errs only against it*. Error too, then, is restricted by the word *only*. The Almighty is saying, as it were, 'There is no greater error than that of him who errs in his knowledge of his own self.' This is the most grievous error, and the worst punishment that can be dealt to a person is to cause him to err from his own self after having known it: *They forgot God, so He made them forget themselves* [Q.LIX.19]. Abū Yazīd al-Bisṭāmī (may God be pleased with him) said, 'I searched for my self in the two realms, but could not find it, until finally I separated from my self, and then I knew who I was.' The Almighty says, *Prosperous is he who purifies* [*his soul*]*; and failed has he who sullies it* [Q.XCI.9–10]. May God grace us with the good of it, and keep us safe from the evil of it, amen!

II

QUESTION: The Shaykh was asked to comment on God's words *Call unto the way of your Lord with wisdom and beautiful counsel, and dispute with them in the most beautiful way* [Q.XVI.125].

ANSWER: When God selects people to deliver his call to mankind, He teaches them the best ways of reminding,[2] so that they draw to themselves the young and the old, the mighty and the humble. Their words are accepted by those who hear them, because it is clear that

1 The Shaykh bases this interpretation on the ambiguity of the particle *li*, which can mean 'to' or 'for.' Ordinarily in this verse, it would be interpreted as 'for': *He who is guided is guided only for himself*, i.e. for his own sake; but according to the Shaykh's understanding here, it may be interpreted as *He who is guided is guided only to himself*.
2 Meaning: reminding people of the Truth.

their words come from the heart, not from books; and when speech comes from the heart, it enters other hearts. Because of this, their counsel affects the hearts of those who hear it, and their allusions take root in their disciples. The masters have understood from this holy verse that people are of three types—and the Prophet (may God bless him and grant him peace) said, 'Put people in their proper places.'

The first of these three types are those who are only drawn by discourse which is marked by wisdom (*ḥikma*); they are the elite among God's servants. The second type are those who are drawn by beautiful counsel (*mawʿiẓa ḥasana*)which takes a middle position between encouragement and warning; that is, which is given with kindness and delicacy. The third type are those who are inclined to disputation (*mujādala*); it is they who cause most difficulty for spiritual guides, whether prophets or saints. God permitted the Prophet to dispute with them, but specified that it be done in the most beautiful way, and then the next most beautiful, and so on. This is why the sword is always the last resort of dispute. Now when anyone contravenes this divinely-sanctioned way of giving counsel, he is almost always rejected. All of this can be inferred from the words of the Prophet (may God bless him and grant him peace), 'Whoso commands, let him command in the best way'; that is, with gentleness and delicacy, so that it is more likely to be accepted. God knows best.

12

QUESTION: The Shaykh was asked to comment on God's words *Invoke your Lord when you forget* [Q.XVIII.24].

ANSWER: This refers to when you are heedless; as for when you have presence of mind, you must be detached from the invocation and immersed in the Invoked. The purpose of invocation is to bring an end to forgetfulness. Thus, when there is forgetfulness, there must be invocation; and when there is awareness, there will be presence.

13

QUESTION: The Shaykh was asked to comment on God's words *Hasten not with the Qur'ān until its revelation has been perfected unto you* [Q.XX.114].

ANSWER: According to the spiritual allusion, this prohibition of haste pertains to the exegesis of the Qur'ān's meanings. The Almighty is saying, as it were, 'Do not hasten, O Muḥammad, in explaining all the meanings of the Qur'ān before their proper time has come: *Nor is there anything but with Us are the treasuries thereof, and We send it not down save in known measure* [Q.XV.21]. Even if the Qur'ān has been completely revealed to you in terms of its laws, it has not been completed in terms of the many inspirations it contains. You are only permitted to disclose what needs to be disclosed; as for its other more mysterious meanings, leave them for their appropriate times. God will bring them to light via those of your community endowed with knowledge.' Someone expressed this truth by saying, 'The truth flows on the tongues of those endowed with knowledge in every era, according to the needs of its people.'

By 'those endowed with knowledge' (*ʿulamā'*) here is meant those with knowledge of God, of whom the following *ḥadīth* speaks, 'The *ʿulamā'* are the heirs of the prophets.' The fact that he said 'the heirs of the prophets' and not 'the heirs of the messengers' indicates to us that they are instructed to keep within the limits of what the Qur'ān contains.[1] What this means is that the inspiration (*ilhām*) which the Real grants them—which is one of the forms of revelation (*waḥy*)—comes to them within the limits of the Qur'ān and not from outside it. They continue (may God be pleased with them) to

1 Islam distinguishes between the messenger (*rasūl*), who founds a religion, and the prophet (*nabī*), who follows a religion founded by a previous messenger. Every messenger is also considered a prophet, but not every prophet is a messenger. Moses was a messenger, whilst David was a prophet since he followed the Law of Moses.

extract extraordinary meanings from the Qur'ān, all of which are effects of the original revelation and its rays, which shine upon their hearts from the Prophetic Presence (*al-ḥaḍra al-nabawiyya*). Thus they will continue to dispense the wonders of the Qur'ān which the Real grants them, until God inherits the earth and all who dwell upon it. The meanings of the Qur'ān are never exhausted, as is implied by the words of the Prophet (may God bless him and grant him peace), 'The wonders of the Qur'ān never cease.'

14

QUESTION: Concerning God's words *Have not the unbelievers seen that the heavens and the earth were of one piece? Then We rifted them asunder, and from the water We made every living thing* [Q.XXI.30], where was the substance of the water when the heavens and the earth were of one piece, i.e. one substance fastened together? Was the substance of the water part of their substance, or separate from them? And was the substance of our life already within it, since He says *and from the water We made every living thing*?

ANSWER: In the Name of God, and may blessings be upon the Prophet. My brother, the holy verse is not concerned with the primordial substance (*awwal al-mawād*), but was revealed in the context of an argument for the existence of a divine Director (*Mudabbir*) against those who deny it. This is why it is addressed to *the unbelievers*, i.e. those who do not believe in the Director of the universe, and not to the believers. In any case, I shall comment on the verse itself; and all clarity comes from God.

Every verse has a near meaning, a nearer meaning, a far meaning and a farther meaning; these four perspectives are alluded to in a *ḥadīth* by the terms 'outward' (*ẓāhir*), 'inward' (*bāṭin*), 'boundary' (*ḥadd*) and 'horizon' (*maṭlaʿ*). The 'nearest' meaning of this verse, the one which is easily understood by all, is that *the heavens and the earth were of one piece*, and then the heavens were separated with rain, and the earth with vegetation. *Verily, in this there are signs* [Q.x.67]. There are traditions to support this interpretation.

There are also traditions to support the second interpretation, which is that the heavens, earth and their contents were *of one piece*, that is, gathered in a single substance, and then were split. This is what Ibn ʿAbbās (may God be pleased with him) is reported to have said, and it has been the opinion of many scholars over the ages, that the nature (*sunna*) of how things are brought forth by the divine Power is as archetypes and then as particulars.

Yet if we follow the interpretation of Ibn ʿAbbās, it is not clear why this should be addressed to *the unbelievers* in general, since they are unaware of what went on when the world was created; although it could indeed be addressed to the wise among them. God guides whom He wills to that wherein is goodness, so that the overwhelming proofs may be on His side. It may be that the divine Wisdom decreed that the meanings of this verse be reserved for the later generations, because its content was destined to be confirmed by those to whom it was addressed thanks to their investigations into the beauty of the universe, which led them to the knowledge that separation follows unity, and that all things were once gathered together before they were separated.[1] This is something to which only the elites of each group have access; for the rest, it was enough for Him to alert them to the general principle of causality, along the lines of His words *Have they not beheld the camel—how it was created?* [Q.LXXXVIII.17], and the like.

Moreover, I say that this verse contains an allusion to the knowledge that non-Muslims have attained, such as astronomy and the secrets of the universe they have discovered, to the extent that they have become certain that all things were originally one substance, which then separated and multiplied. It is my view that this verse is one the miracles of the Qur'ān because of how direct it is in its subject matter, which those whom it addresses have come to learn. It is our

1 The Shaykh is referring to what is now commonly known as the 'Big Bang.'

view that we should acknowledge all the information they possess, save for that which has to do with religion such as their denial of certain truths and other necessary elements of faith. Of these latter, they are ignorant, although they do have knowledge of other things, as the Qur'ān itself says, *They know only an outward appearance of this lower life; of the hereafter, they are oblivious* [Q.xxx.7].

What we said about the verse having an allusion to the knowledge attained by those it addresses can be inferred from the rhetorical question: *Have not the unbelievers seen...?* Rhetorical questions are only asked of things which the addressee acknowledges to be true. The fact that the verse says *seen* and not *known* points to the accuracy of their discovery. The Almighty is saying as it were: Has it not been clearly established by the unbelievers that the heavens and the earth were of one piece, i.e. a single substance (everyone has their own technical term for it), after which He separated them completely—do you not see who it was who caused this one piece to exist, and who caused it then to split from the composition in which it appeared to be? My suspicion is that if any honest person kindles even the smallest of torches from the flame of his thought, and uses it to examine the way in which the elements of the world are composed, he will not hesitate to say *Hallowed be God, the Best of creators!* [Q.xxiii.14]. He will say this because of the beautiful order he beholds, and the magnificent arrangement, measure and supreme balance by which all things are flawlessly weighed.

Ages and years have passed, and nights and days have succeeded one another, yet in all this time the celestial bodies have continued in their motion without interruption or collision, *Each in an orbit glides onwards* [Q.xxxvi.40]. Glory be to Him who *raised the heavens aloft and set the balance* [Q.lv.7] so that neither scale outweighs the other. This is not merely a balance for the weighing of oats and barley; it is far nobler and loftier than that, and perhaps it is the means by which the substances of the world are kept in place, and by which all things are set in their place—that is, by which they are balanced. Do you not see who designed this and wound it up, and prevented the universe from clashing with itself or straying from its position? *Were [the heavens and earth] to deviate, there is not one who could grasp them in His stead* [Q.XXXV.41].

Now they might say that it is but gravity that naturally causes all things to remain in their positions or follow their orbits. To this, I say: Who designed gravity and set down the balance, and linked effects to their causes? Need anything else be said? Indeed, the honest and fair unbeliever needs even less than this to affirm the existence of the Creator; yet *If one should go astray, you shall find no guiding ally* [Q.XVIII.17].

As for His words *and from the water We made every living thing*, what was said above also applies to them, and their literal meaning is not unclear. The Almighty says, *He sends down water from the sky by which He gives life to the earth after its death* [Q.XXX.24]. Thus everything that has life draws the substance of its life, and the sustenance of its existence, from water. Animals and plants are equal in this respect; indeed, they are all plants, for the Almighty says, *God brought you out of the earth, growing* [Q.LXXI.17]. From this perspective, animals and plants are equal; everything on earth that has a body that grows can be considered a plant, and then from this general class animals are a specific group, namely that which grows by being separate from the earth and drawing substance from what lies above it, whilst everything else is rooted in the earth and draws sustenance from what is beneath it. An animal is nothing but a tree that has been separated from the earth, which sometimes moves by its own volition and sometimes by compulsion; a tree is nothing but an animal which is rooted in the earth and has no free will, but is nevertheless not denied its own share of *tawḥīd* and faith: God says, *The star and the tree bow down* [Q.LV.6].

Now since we see that all living things on earth are plants, and that plants cannot do without water, it becomes clear to us that water is the life of all growing bodies. What is meant here is the life of the physical body, or we might say the life of this world, which means the connection of the spirit to the body to which God refers when he says,

Give them the parable of the life of this world: it is like water We send from the sky, so that the plants of the earth mingle with it; and in the morning it is straw scattered by the winds [Q.XVIII.45]. As for life in and of itself, before it is connected to the body, it has no need for material things which are subject to decay. Thus we may say that matter is necessary for life to remain in the body, but not for life itself to exist, since it existed before all bodies; a *ḥadīth* says that 'God created the spirits a thousand years before the bodies.' The span of time here is only meant to tell us that subtle being existed before gross being, and that this is the way of God in His creation, to which He alludes by saying, *God is He who sends forth the winds that stir up clouds, which He spreads in the sky as He will, and shatters them; then you see rain coming forth from the midst of them* [Q.XXX.48]. Every cause is subtler than its effect: the wind causes the clouds to exist, and the clouds cause the rain to exist, and the rain causes the plants to exist, and the plants cause the animals to be sustained—and God is the Cause of all causes, and all things go back to Him.

As for your question about the substance of the water, and whether it was interconnected with the substance of the heavens and the earth, I say: The unity of the beginning is established, just as the precedence of the subtle over the gross is established. Now the most subtle and influential of all the elements is the element of ether, which the ancients called the element of fire; then come the elements of wind, then water and then earth. Each lower element is composed of those above it, and proceeds from it, and each composition is under the power of those from which it is composed. Earth proceeds from the three elements of water, wind and ether, and is therefore under their power. Water is under the power of wind because it proceeds from it, and under examination can be seen to be composed of it and of what comes before it; this is why it becomes one with air when it evaporates. This is the way of God, *As We began the first creation, so shall We return it* [Q.XXI.104]. Wind is under the power of ether because it proceeds from it, and that may be so by means of the Spirit. [As for] the Spirit, it cannot be fathomed by the mind, *They ask you about the Spirit. Say, 'The Spirit proceeds from the command of my Lord; and you have not been given knowledge, save but a little* [Q.XVII.85]. All guidance comes from God, and He is our sufficiency and the best of trustees.

15

QUESTION: God says, *And Dhul-Nūn, when he went forth enraged and thought that We would have no power over him; then he called out in the darkness, 'There is no god but You. Glory be to You, I have been an evildoer!'* [Q.XXI.87]. Does this verse mean that Jonah (upon whom be peace) had doubts in his mind about the power of the All-Powerful?

ANSWER: Far be it for any prophet to doubt in the Almighty's power! The words *and [he] thought that We would have no power over him* mean that he thought God would not restrict him, as in His words *He whose provision is restricted, let him spend from what God has given him* [Q.LXV.7].[1] Now since God is 'as His believing servant thinks of Him',[2] Jonah's suspicion profited him; for as you know, God saved him from the belly of the Whale. Had he not thought the best of God, he would have remained in its belly until the Day of Resurrection.

16

QUESTION: What is the esoteric way of understanding God's words, *Have you not looked to your Lord—how He stretches out the shadow? If He willed, He would make it unmoving. Then We make the sun a guide to it, and then We draw it to Ourselves, drawing it gently* [Q.XXV.45-46]?

ANSWER: The way to understand a statement may be determined by considering those to whom it is addressed. Without doubt, these words were not merely meant to inspire the addressee to reflect on a particular divine act and the wisdom of it, since it is possible that the addressee was already aware of this. Of course, there are some people who

1 The verb used here to 'restrict' is *qadar ʿalā*, which also means 'to have power over'.
2 Allusion to a sacred *ḥadīth*.

understand these verse in this way; but as for the spiritual elite, they might focus on the words *Have you not looked to your Lord*, and understand from this that the Real is inspiring them to behold the Cause before the effects. Along these lines, it is related that the greatest witness of truth (*al-ṣiddīq al-akbar*)[1] said, 'I never saw anything without seeing God before it.'

Others among the spiritual elite might see that He is inspiring them to behold how the shadow is stretched out, and whence its substance comes[2]—for it is He who stretches out the shadow. Thus their sight goes back and forth between the 'how' and the substance, and their insight penetrates to what lies beyond the 'how', and they find that there is no 'how' at all, since it is unique and not preceded by any modality. One such as these says, 'I never saw anything without seeing God with it'; and some of them understand this according to the true 'with-ness' (*maʿiyya*) affirmed by God's words *And He is with you wherever you are* [Q.LVII.4].

Then there are those whose sight falls first on the shadow; this is the perspective of the masses, who see effects as proof of the Cause, and shadows as proof of the one who casts them. One such as these says, 'I never saw anything without seeing God after it.' When his eyes fall upon a shadow, he inevitably looks towards the thing casting the shadow, whatever it may be, since a shadow cannot exist by itself or be separated from that which casts it. Now such a person may move up to the state wherein he sees the object casting the shadow without needing to see the shadow first, which is implied by His words *If He willed, He would make it unmoving*, or by His words *then We draw it to Ourselves*; for a shadow is nothing but an ascending path which leads one's sight to the object which casts it.

As for His words *If He willed, He would make it unmoving*, they mean: If He willed, He would cause it to remain on the level of

1 Meaning Abū Bakr al-Ṣiddīq the Companion of the Prophet and first caliph.
2 The Shaykh is playing with the correspondence between the verb *madda*, 'to stretch out', and the noun *mādda*, 'substance', which have the same lexical root.

divine Knowledge, rather than the level of visible existence, or we might say measured existence. Yet He did not will this, but instead made *the sun a guide to it*. On this level, the *sun* is nothing other than the emanation of the pure light to which He alludes when He says, *God is the light of the heavens and the earth* [Q.XXIV.35]. It is this light that gives being to nonexistent things and measures them out; its role, according to this perspective, is to determine the measure of things just as the sun determines one's shadow and controls its modality and movement, lengthening and shortening it as it comes and goes. It is the sun which gives the object this; the shadow does not create itself, nor does the object which casts it, since the true nature of both of them cannot change. The form of the object is fixed in its point of existence, and the form of the shadow is fixed in its form of nonexistence; the sun is what causes them to change in appearance and motion. This does not mean that the object casting the shadow actually changes, or that the shadow itself has a free will of its own.

I say, moreover, that the shadow requires three fundamentals in order to exist. The first fundamental is an object which exists in and of itself and which casts the shadow. According to this perspective, this can be nothing other than the Real, because His Being is not drawn from the being of anything else.

The second fundamental is the plane upon which the shadow is cast. This can be nothing other than All-Possibility (*al-imkān*); this means that every possible thing is only manifested on the plane of All-Possibility.

The third fundamental is the presence of light, because this is what determines the measure of the shadow.

What exists as a potential can only become manifest in an object. This can be nothing other than a particular divine Name, which (according to this perspective) is manifested in a particular way—and not in an absolute way, since that would make it utterly enveloped in the Essence of the Object casting the shadow. It is to this that He alludes when He says, *and then We draw it to Ourselves, drawing it gently*.

In sum, the Beginningless Names[1] give each possibility its existence in the divine Knowledge, and the Endless Names[2] give it its measured existence.[3] Everything has its measure.

I say, moreover, that if this verse was only meant as a literal allusion to the shadows of this world, it would not have called the sun a *guide to it*, since on the contrary it is actually the shadow which is a guide to the sun: note how we use shadows to determine the time of midday, and the like. Why else, then, would the verse call the sun the *guide* to the shadow? Secondly, if He only meant the verse to be literal, He would not have said *then We draw it to Ourselves*, naming Himself as the point to which it is drawn. Thus this verse is governed by His words *All things reach God at last* [Q.XL.53].[4]

17

QUESTION: The Shaykh was asked about the words of Abraham, as reported in the Qur'ān: *And confer on me a worthy repute among the latter folk* [Q.XXVI.84].

ANSWER: The *latter folk* here means the community of Muḥammad, since his prayer was answered in them. I do not know of any community who holds him in as high repute as he merits, save for this blessed one. This is because he brought forth a strange tiding: *When the night grew dark upon him he beheld a planet, and said: 'This is my Lord'* [Q.VI.76] and so on; and this tiding was not received favourably by the minds of the weak, and *They gave the lie to that which they could not comprehend* [Q.X.39] because they were unable to digest such truths. Therefore they turned away from him, after having followed him at first. And so he said, 'Lord, *confer on me a worthy repute among the latter folk*', that I not be reviled as I was by the earlier folk.

1 *Al-Asmā' al-Azaliyya*, the divine Names on the level of the Essence.
2 *Al-Asmā' al-Abadiyya*, the divine Names on the level of creation or manifestation.
3 That is, its existence in the manifested world.
4 This paragraph provides the Shaykh's justification for interpreting the verse mystically.

Then the Prophet (may God bless him and grant him peace) was sent forth, bringing with him the way (*millat*) of our master Abraham,[1] and his community knew the true meaning of his words, *This is my Lord*, and interpreted them in the proper way, and believed him [Abraham] in what he saw. Now do not think, my brother, that when our master Abraham said *This is my Lord* he was ignorant of the truth of divinity; far from it! He was immersed in the glory of God Almighty, and saw Him in all things. When he gave voice to this great blessing, his people decried him; and therefore he said, *I turn my face towards Him who created the heavens and the earth, a man of pure faith. I am no idolater* [Q.VI.79].

(The questioner said, 'Shaykh, when our master Abraham (upon whom be peace) said *This is my Lord*, was he unaware of the true status of divinity?')

Far from it! Rather, he was totally immersed in the glory of God. Now we know that the prophets are divinely protected from all sins, major and minor, both before their prophethood begins and after it; how, then, could any of them display ignorance of the true status of divinity? This becomes clearer when we consider that the occasion when he said *This is my Lord* actually took place after the dominions of heaven and earth had been revealed to him, as God says, *Thus did We show unto Abraham the dominion of the heavens and of the earth, that he might be of those possessing certainty* [Q.VI.75].

Indeed, it was this very *certainty* that made him say *This is my Lord*. As the saying goes, 'When certainty (*īqān*) comes, one witnesses first-hand (*ʿiyān*) that there is no multiplicity (*aʿyān*).' Thus, with the insight of faith he saw the presence of the Real in every direction and every place, and divulged this secret with a cry of *This is my Lord!* In saying this, he desired to raise his people through the ranks of faith to the highest level of spiritual excellence (*iḥsān*); but they preferred to cling to the ground.[2]

1 Allusion to Qur'ānic verses like: II.135, III.95, IV.125, etc

2 Allusion to Qur'ānic verse VII.176: *And had We willed We could have raised him by their means [Our revelations], but he clung to the earth and followed his own lust.*

18

QUESTION: God says, *Verily, prayer prevents iniquity and abomination, but the remembrance of God is greater* [Q.XXIX.45]. How is it that remembrance is greater, even through prayer (*ṣalāt*) itself contains remembrance, supplication and so on? What exactly is 'remembrance' (*dhikr*)?

ANSWER: The meaning of this (and God knows best) is that prayer prevents iniquity and abomination, whether it be offered with presence of mind or without it; but to remember God in prayer—that is, for the one who prays to remember that he is with God, whether he is merely aware of His presence, or actually beholds Him—is greater in its prevention of them. So the meaning goes back to prayer itself, and not to something outside of it; and God knows best.[1]

19

QUESTION: The Shaykh was asked to comment on God's words, *God is He who created the heavens and the earth, and all that is between them, in six days* [Q.XXXII.4].

ANSWER: Before an action is done, it is identical with its agent; after it is done, it becomes an attribute of its agent. Either way, it is part of what makes the nature of the agent complete. Now all things came from the divine Knowledge, which has the attribute of beginninglessness (*qidam*); it is a curious wonder that this level is called nothingness (*ʿadam*). That all things were always contained

1 Elsewhere, the Shaykh said, 'Remembrance is the mightiest rule of the religion… The law was not enjoined upon us, neither were the rites of worship ordained but for the sake of establishing the remembrance of God… In a word, our performance of the rites of worship is considered strong or weak according to the degree of our remembrance of God while performing them.' Lings, *A Sufi Saint*, pp. 96-97.

in the divine Knowledge is something that anyone who has the least bit of understanding is able to sense. This was the first day of the six days of God in which He created the heavens and the earth. All things existed only as the contents of the beginningless Knowledge, in which they were completely enveloped.

Now the second day refers to the turning of the divine Will to all things; for without doubt, they are contained in the Will of God, and what God wills, is.

Then, after the Will, the divine Speech becomes attached to them, *His command, when He wills a thing, is but to say to it 'Be!', and it is* [Q.XXXVI.82]. This represents the third day.

Then, after the word *Be!*, they are transferred to the divine Power, which brings them into the fourth of the days of God: if the Power brings something into existence, it exists; and if it does not, then it does not.

Then the divine Hearing and Sight become attached to them, because they cannot be attached to something that does not exist. These represent the fifth and sixth days. Thus, all things are contained and revealed, *Then He said to them and to the earth, 'Come forth, willingly or unwillingly!' They said, 'We come forth willingly'* [Q.XLI.11].

Now the use of the word 'day' to mean 'quality' (*ṣifa*) is something that is found in the Words of God; one example is found in His words, *Remind them of the days of God* [Q.XIV.5], that is, the Qualities of God, according to one exegete (who was one of God's Folk). Clearly the use of the word 'day' is a way of incorporating the two meanings; but the less immediate meaning is more important and appropriate for this level, since it is being used in the context of the time before the day had yet been created. The day, after all, is a span of time determined by the motion of the heavenly bodies. This is why He says *the days of God* rather than 'the days of this world'. [Ḥaqqī] says in *Rūḥ al-bayān*: 'In reality, the days of God are those in which 'God was, and there was nothing with Him',[1] neither the days of this world, nor the days of the hereafter. The spiritual wayfarer should reflect on this, and ponder how he is a treasure of God's Knowledge; he should leave this symbolic world, restricted by day and night, for the real world wherein there is neither day nor night.'

What this means is that we should pay attention to how, as we said, all beings in existence are contained in the Beginningless Quality, and we should be certain that they have no being whatsoever outside the realms of the Six Qualities.[2] As for Life,[3] since it has no direct object on the level of possibilities, it is not given alongside the other six; yet it too has its place, represented by the 'settling' when He says, *Then He settled above the Throne* [Q.XXXII.4].[4] God knows best.

20

QUESTION: The Shaykh was asked about God's words, about David (upon whom be peace), *We strengthened his kingdom, and gave him wisdom and discernment in speech* [Q.XXXVIII.20].[5]

ANSWER: These words sound glorious to the ear, and the soul instinctively feels their weight without having to consider their meaning, because of the dread and gravity they evoke. Indeed, these words have such profuse meanings that one might find it difficult to pin down exactly what they mean. It concerns us not that some exegetes consider this to refer to the idiom *ammā baʿd*,[6] since others say that it means that speech wherein there is no ambiguity whatsoever because of how the speaker pays close attention

1 *Ḥadīth*.
2 Knowledge, Will, Speech, Power, Hearing and Sight.
3 The seventh of the 'Affirmative Qualities' (*ṣifāt thubūtiyya*) in Ashʿarī theology.
4 This corresponds to the 'seventh day.'
5 The question concerns these last words, *faṣl al-khiṭāb*, 'discernment in speech'; the word *faṣl* literally means to cut, to divide, to render judgement.
6 An Arabic idiom used in speeches to separate the preamble from the main content, literally meaning 'As for what follows...'

to how he arranges his words in terms of pauses, continuations, word order, sentence structure, directness, allusion, elision and repetition. It could also be said that it means speech that is decisive and to the point, being neither too brief nor too prolix, as is always the case with the speech of prophets. This is the best explanation.

As for Fakhr al-Dīn Rāzī, he gave an even simpler explanation in his exegesis, saying, 'People have different levels of ability to express what is in their minds. Some are unable to arrange their words properly at all, so that everything they say is confused. Others have certain deficiencies in their ability to arrange their words. Others are able to say precisely what they mean and express it to the utmost degree of clarity. Those whose ability in this regard is closer to perfection will have a greater impact when they speak what is on their mind; those whose ability in this regard is further from perfection will have a weaker impact when they speak. Now when God proclaimed the perfection of the content of David's mind by saying *and [We] gave him wisdom*, He followed this by proclaiming the perfection of his spoken words and expressions by saying *and discernment in speech*. This arrangement of words is as glorious as can be.'

I say that the words *discernments in speech* have a profusion of meanings, and that this is certainly one of them, inasmuch as God utters them in the course of speaking of David's special distinctions. Yet the context in which they are uttered implies that they are closely related to power and wisdom, since the Almighty says *We strengthened his kingdom, and gave him wisdom and discernment in speech*; it seems unlikely to us that the third item in this list could mean anything other than something that closely accords with the first two. This is what occurs to us, and God knows best.

21

QUESTION: How do the spiritual masters understand God's words *The retribution for an evil is an evil like it* [Q.XLII.40]?

ANSWER: When it comes to understanding this verse, people are of three types. The first type infer from it that it is permitted for a person who has been wronged to exact retribution from the one who wronged him, *Whoso aggresses against you, aggress against him even as he aggresses against you* [Q.II.194]. This is the understanding of most people.

The second type understand that it permits retribution, but restricts it to like-for-like—and it is usually impossible for a man to claim the exact retribution the law allows him without exceeding it in the least. Indeed, the retribution is usually greater than the original crime. Thus fearing that they will not be able to keep within God's bounds, these people prefer the way of patience. This is the understanding of the elite among the Muslims.

The third type do not even consider retribution, seeing it to be evil. After all, God says *the recompense for an evil is an evil like it*; that is, the retribution is just as evil as the sin itself. Given this, *whoso pardons and puts things right, his wage falls upon God* [Q.XLII.40].

22

QUESTION: When God says *We have given you a clear victory* [Q.XLVIII.1], does this refer to the conquest of Mecca, the story of the Ḥudaybiyya Truce (as most exegetes say), or something on a higher plane than either?

ANSWER: The fact God explains these words by saying immediately after them *That God may forgive you...* [Q.XLVIII.2], means that the explanation of the 'victory' given by some exegetes is insufficient. What does forgiveness have to do with the conquest of Mecca or any other city? Had He meant the conquest of Mecca, He would have said, 'That God might establish you in a position of power upon the earth', or 'That God might succour you', or the like. Therefore we must interpret this 'victory' as a reference to the Supreme Victory (*al-fatḥ al-akbar*), which is altogether more fitting for this context. It means nothing other than the victory of the inner eye (*baṣīra*) and the establishment of the heart in the vision of the Almighty Real. Now since a victory can be unclear[1]—and indeed this is to be expected, since a veil often falls back into place after being lifted—God specified that this was a clear victory, *We have given you a clear victory*, certain to be preserved from the intrusion of any blemishes or setbacks that might otherwise have been feared.

'And We only gave you this clear victory, O Muḥammad, in order *that God might forgive you your former sin*.' This refers to the sin for which the Prophet (may God bless him and grant him peace) would ask forgiveness by saying such things as, 'Glory be to You, I have wronged myself and done evil, so forgive me, for none can forgive sins but You!' Now the believer might find it far-fetched—and indeed unimaginable—that the Prophet (may God bless him and grant him peace) could commit sin. But the Prophet had total knowledge of his own self; otherwise, he would not have asked forgiveness of God.

Let me mention to you something about this matter that God showed to me. I say that the Prophet (may God bless him and grant him peace) was obliged to believe in his message just as all others were; God alluded to this when He said, *The messenger believes in what has been revealed to him from his Lord* [Q.II.285]. Because of this, when he came to know of his own message, it occurred to him that he had been guilty of a shortcoming against his own self, since he had treated himself with no special esteem and seen himself as nothing more than Muḥammad ibn ʿAbd Allāh. Now there is no doubt that if a man is in the company of a messenger of God but does not know him to be such, he will fall short of the proper etiquette that such a situation demands. Then when he is told that his companion is actually a messenger of God, he will realise all the gaffes and slips he was making before, and will feel so ashamed of this that he will turn to God Almighty and ask His forgiveness for these shortcomings.

1 Meaning: it can be an incomplete victory.

So it was with the Prophet (may God bless him and grant him peace), who saw himself as nothing more than a man named Muḥammad ibn ʿAbd Allāh; and then when God opened the eye of his heart and showed him who he really was, and the respect he owed to himself as a Heaven-sent messenger just as respect was owed to him by others, he said, 'I have wronged myself.' That is, I wronged my own self before by not giving it its due: I did not acknowledge its prophethood, or that it is the noblest of all creation. Thus God said to him, 'We only gave you this clear victory so that God might forgive you for this former sin and for any remnant of it there might be in the future.' He had underestimated his own self and perhaps even held it in low esteem, and God informed him that He had pardoned him for doing so. And since the Prophet (may God bless him and grant him peace) might have imagined that the favour was incomplete, He told him that He had only given him this clear victory in order *that He might complete his favour unto you and guide you to a straight path; and that God might help you with mighty help* [Q.XLVIII.2–3].

So we should understand from this that all of these things—forgiveness of sins, travel on the path of guidance, divine help and a goodly end—are connected to the clear victory. If God gives someone the victory of the gnostics and spiritual heirs, he should not doubt that he has been forgiven, aided and guided. If anyone strays from the path, it is because his victory was not a clear one; it is to this that God alludes when He says, *The final end is for the righteous* [Q.VII.128].

23

QUESTION: The Shaykh was asked about the story of the Chapter of 'The Star' and the manner in which it was revealed, and of the so-called 'Sacred Birds' (*gharānīq*) and the 'Satanic Verses.'[1]

ANSWER: Contrary to the usual form the Revelation took, the

1 In brief, the story—which is mentioned not in the major books of *ḥadīth* but rather in some of the classical commentaries on the Qur'ān, whose authors generally collected everything which had reached their ears about a particular verse of Qur'ān without comment or discrimination—states that when the Prophet first recited the Chapter of 'The Star' to Quraysh at the Kaᶜba, when he reached the verses, *Have you seen, then, al-Lāt and al-ᶜUzzā, and Manāt, the third, the other?* (Q.LIII.19-20), Satan cast into his heart a false inspiration which made him then utter, 'These are the Sacred Birds, and their intercession is much sought' (*tilka 'l-gharānīqu wa-shafāᶜatuhum turjā*). Quraysh interpreted this to mean that the three goddesses mentioned in these verses had been accepted by Islam as intermediaries between God and man, and thus rejoiced and fell down in prostration along with the Prophet and the Muslims. The Prophet and the Muslims had prostrated themselves as the final verse of 'The Star' is: *Bow down (or prostrate yourself) and worship God.* See note below on the Verses of Prostration. Soon after, however, God inspired the Prophet with the verses which actually were meant to follow verse 20: *What, have you males, and He females? That were indeed an unjust division. They are but names you have named—you and your fathers; God has send down no authority for them* (Q.LIII.21-23). Thus were the false verses expunged and replaced with the correct ones, to the dismay of the pagans of Quraysh, who had seen the event as the kind of compromise for which they had been hoping. The story is rejected by most exegetes as uncorroborated and somewhat fantastical even as they relate it (cf. Nasafī, Bayḍāwī, Ibn Kathīr, Qurṭubī, Rāzī, Nīsāpūrī, etc.), but the nature of classical Qur'ānic exegesis, based as it often is on the indiscriminate narration of every tradition or story connected with a verse, sometimes without any comment from the exegete, has meant that the story has remained in the Muslim consciousness to this day. Salman Rushdie's controversial novel *The Satanic Verses*, which includes a fictionalized portrayal of the event in question, brought this matter to the attention of the West upon release of the novel in 1988; before this, it had been a matter of interest only to orientalists and Arabists. The Shaykh al-ᶜAlawī's comments here were made some fifty years before this novel was written and thus naturally pertain to the question of the original alleged incident, not to the controversy aroused by the novel; I have nevertheless retained the phrase 'Satanic Verses' because it has become familiar to the Western reader.

Chapter of 'The Star' was revealed to our master Muḥammad all at once,[1] thus seizing him from without and from within, and marking him according to his true rank in his Lord's sight. How could it be otherwise, when it made a proclamation so dear to mankind, namely the true noble status of the Prophet and the subtle and sublime secret of his inner relationship to God Almighty, and how he came near to Him and approached Him? Thus it is that whosoever reflects upon this Chapter might almost fall down in prostration even before he reaches its final verse.[2]

Because of this, the Prophet hoped that if he recited this Chapter to the idolaters it might be enough to put an end to idolatry and replace it with the doctrine of divine Unity, so he went to them with this hope burning brightly in his soul. But Satan (God curse him) cast doubt upon his hope, *Yet God abolishes that which Satan casts; then God establishes His revelations* [Q.XXII.52].

The Prophet entered the Sanctuary where Quraysh were in attendance, accompanied by a group of his followers. He saw that if 'The Star' were recited even to Satan he would fall prostrate because of the dazzling truths and overwhelming power it contained; and thus it proved.

For when the Prophet recited it, and it captivated the very being of all who heard it, he fell prostrate along with his followers; and the idolaters followed them in prostration, not knowing why the Revelation had overpowered them so. Seeing this, the believers were struck with amazement by their [the idolaters'] prostration, and the Prophet's hopes intensified that the idolaters might become believers. Yet:

> A man will not always find what he hopes for:
> The winds often blow where the ships need them least.[3]

1 That is, it was not revealed in piecemeal form as even some of the shorter Chapters were.

2 The final verse of 'The Star' is one of the so-called 'Verses of Prostration' (*āyāt al-sajda*) of the Qur'ān, those verses upon the recital of which the Muslim who utters them or hears them uttered must prostrate himself.

3 A famous verse of al-Mutanabbī.

And God Almighty says in this very Chapter, *Or shall a man have whatever he hopes for?* [Q.LIII.24]. That is, he shall not have whatever he hopes for. Therefore the throne of Satan shuddered as they prostrated, and he inspired one of the idolaters to claim, 'I only prostrated because when the Prophet reached the verses *Have you seen, then, Al-Lāt, and Al-ʿUzzā, and Manāt the third, the other?*, I heard the words, "These are the Sacred Birds, and their intercession is much sought," and I prostrated upon hearing this.' When the other idolaters heard the man say this, they all adopted the same claim, saying, 'We only prostrated for this reason,' thereby seeking to support their own doctrine; for they felt that their prostration alongside our master Muḥammad had been a shameful thing. And when they capitulated in this way, the Prophet's hope for them faded because he had expected otherwise; and the pure joy of the gathering faded and his hopes in them were dashed, and he fell into a sombre mood, remaining thus until God consoled him and alleviated his sorrow by saying to him, *And never sent We a messenger nor prophet before you save that, when he hoped, Satan cast (doubt) upon his hope. Yet God abolishes that which Satan casts; then God establishes His revelations. And God is Knowing, Wise*[1] [Q.XXII.52].

That is, this is the Way of God (*Sunnat Allāh*) with His creatures: whenever a prophet or messenger had a hope—and none of them hoped for anything save that for which Muḥammad hoped, namely for his people to embrace faith—Satan cast doubt on his hopes, so that which was pure became turbid, and the truth became mixed with false-

1 This is the Shaykh al-ʿAlawī's interpretation of this Qur'ānic verse; the verb *tamannā*, translated here as 'hoped', is usually interpreted as meaning 'recited', and the word *umniyatih*, here translated as 'his hope', is usually interpreted as meaning 'that which he recited' (the Arabic language allows both possibilities; indeed the most common meaning of *tamannā* is 'to hope'). Thus the Shaykh al-ʿAlawī affirms that it was not the verses of the Qur'ān revealed to the Prophet that were 'touched' by Satan, but rather the interpretation of these verses in the minds of the idolaters, who sought to excuse themselves for being unable to resist the power of the Qur'ān and thus prostrating. This means that Satan did not 'cast a false revelation' into the Prophet's heart, but rather he 'cast doubt' on the hopes of the Prophet for the conversion of the Qurayshi pagans.

hood. Yet God always abolished what Satan casts, and then established His revelations, as He says, *Lo! We have sent down this Remembrance; and lo! We are its Guardian* [Q.XV.9].

24

QUESTION: According to the Qur'ān, the Disciples [of Christ] said, *We are God's helpers* [Q.LXI.14]. Was God not free from any need for their help?

ANSWER: The words of the Disciples give us a sense of their broad knowledge and perfect trust in God's bounty, and their confidence that God requites actions in kind. Without doubt, they were in dire need of God's help for themselves, and therefore they said *We are God's helpers* so that God would say in turn 'I am your Helper.' *If you help God, He will help you* [Q. XLVII.7].

[On another occasion, the Shaykh answered the same question by saying:] The words of the Disciples *We are God's helpers* indicate the vastness of their mystical knowledge and their firm grasp of Pure Oneness (*al-tawḥīd al-maḥḍ*); for they were spoken in response to Christ's words *Who are my helpers unto God?*, ascribing the help to himself, to which the Disciples answered, *We are God's Helpers*. This resembles the words of ʿĀ'isha (may God be pleased with her), 'I thank no one but God.'

25

QUESTION: The Shaykh was asked about *Sūrat al-Māʿūn*, which begins: *Have you seen him who belies the Religion?* [Q.CVII.1].

ANSWER: God's words, *Have you seen him who belies the Religion* essentially mean, 'Do you who is being addressed know who belies the Religion, i.e. the Day of Judgement?'[1] Thus it would be plausible to answer that since belying is an attitude of the heart, it is not possible for one to know who has this attitude unless he first seeks for it in

1 The Day of Religion (*yawn al-dīn*) is another expression for the Day of Judgement.

himself? There must be some kind of sign to identify him, and therefore God says, *That is he who repels the orphan, and urges not the feeding of the needy* [Q.CVII.2–3]. So he who finds these two characteristics in himself, he is one of those who belie the Day of Religion—or may be on the point of becoming one of them—because he perceives no merit in urging the feeding of the needy, nor fears any punishment for driving away orphans.

The question might then arise, 'Even if such a person prays?', and therefore God says, *Woe, then to those who pray yet are unmindful of their prayer* [Q.CVII.5], that is, the purpose of their prayer. *They who make a show* [Q.CVII.6] of their outward deeds, *yet refuse small kindnesses!* [Q.CVII.7] That is, refuse to offer anything of benefit to others. What this means is that those who truly pray are those who neither fret nor withhold; that is, those exempted in God's words, *Man was created fretful: when evil visits him, impatient, and when good visits him, withholding—save for those who pray* [Q.LXX.19–22].

26

QUESTION: The Shaykh was asked about God's words: *Whoso has done an atom's weight of good shall see it; and whoso has done at atom's weight of evil shall see it* [Q.XCIX.7–8].

ANSWER: Pronouns very often have God as their antecedent, especially *anā*, *anta* and *huwa*,[1] which are all true Names of God with which He has named Himself. Because of this, whenever the folk of special understanding find a pronoun, they see its primary and true Antecedent, following it back to this Source with an intellection grasped only by those endowed with innate knowledge. With this in mind, the pronoun *huwa* in the words *shall see it* here refers to God [thus it would

1 'I', 'you' and 'he' or 'it.' Arabic has no neuter or 'non-human' pronoun corresponding to 'it', and thus the word *huwa* could mean either 'he' or 'it' in English.

be better rendered in English as *shall see Him*].[1] It is as though God were saying to those whom He addresses here, 'Whosoever of you does the least amount of sincere good, though it be but an atom's weight, shall see God.' This is a product of the overflowing Grace and Goodness of God, of which the sacred *ḥadīth* states, 'When My servant draws a hand's span nigh unto Me, I draw an arm's length nigh unto Him.'

As for the pronoun in the second verse, *and whoso has done at atom's weight of evil shall see Him*—does this mean that evildoing is a means to attaining the Vision of God? No, but rather it is even more fitting to interpret this pronoun as having God as its antecedent, since the person whom it describes has clearly attained to a high rank indeed: *Whoso has done an atom's weight of evil shall see Him*, that is, the person who has committed no more than an atom's weight of evil shall not be barred from the path to God on account of this evil. Thus the first verse describes the person who has done no good at all, and then begins to strive towards God with fervour and sincerity; the first atom's weight of good he does shall be the means by which he ascends unto the Presence of God. As for the person described in the second verse, he is guilty of no more than an atom's weight of evil, and this evil will not be a barrier to him in his search for God. And God knows best.

Questions and Answers on the Subject of the Ḥadīth

I

QUESTION: The Shaykh was asked about the *ḥadīth*, 'Pray the prayer of one who bids farewell.'

1 This is a clear example of the Shaykh's astonishing ability to penetrate human language and return it again and again to what he sees as the truth which is manifested everywhere, the 'Pure Unity' (*al-tawḥīd al-maḥḍ*) of which he so often speaks. In the pronoun which virtually all Muslims, even esoterists, would consider to refer to the aforementioned *atom's weight* of good or evil, the Shaykh al-ʿAlawī sees the Divine Name *Huwa*, 'He', the ever-present 'warp on which the Qur'ānic text is woven.' (Lings, *A Sufi Saint*, p. 37.)

ANSWER: Praise be to Him who enlightened the inner eyes of the gnostics and made them wellsprings of wisdom and lamps of faith. May blessings and peace be upon him who said, 'Follow my *Sunna* and the *Sunna* of the rightly-guided Caliphs.'

My beloved and righteous friend, you have asked me to share something of the understanding of the gnostics concerning a *ḥadīth* of the Master of Messengers (may God bless him and grant him peace), namely his words, 'Pray the prayer of one who bids farewell, as though you will never pray again.' Now you are well aware that speech differs according to understandings, and that everyone has his station, *All are watered with the same water, yet We favour some over others in flavour* [Q.XIII.4]. When it comes to understanding God's words, people are divided into three types, each one with their own portion. The draught of the elite is too much for the masses to bear; *above everyone who knows, there is one who knows more* [Q.XII.76].

You have no need for me to explain the general understanding of this *ḥadīth*; indeed, you know more about that than we do. But nevertheless we shall say something about it, since other things follow from it. The Messenger of God (may God bless him and grant him peace) would always speak to people according to the capacity of their minds; and minds have varying capacities. The way the masses understand this *ḥadīth* is not the same as the way the elite understand it; each takes what he is able to bear. So in the language of the masses—this is the first interpretation—the *ḥadīth* means: Pray the prayer of one who is bidding farewell, for your continued life is not guaranteed, and this may well be your last prayer. Fix yourself on the possibility of passing away, and pray as well as you can, making sure your prayer is correctly performed in every way, both outwardly and inwardly, with peace, humility, presence of heart and piety. Consider it your final prayer in this life. If you do this, and it becomes your regular habit, then your prayer will be as the Lawgiver commands and as Islam requires. This is the outward meaning of the *ḥadīth* according to the understanding of the masses.

The second interpretation is the understanding of the elite. Someone of this station sees that when the Prophet (may God bless him and grant him peace) tells him to pray the prayer of one who is bidding farewell, he means: Pray without seeing yourself pray, because the one who bids farewell to his prayer offers it without regarding it, and without even considering it to exist. He is lost in the vision of its content as it flows over him; he neither relies on it nor derives support from it, to the point where it is as though he did not even pray it. This is why the Prophet said 'as though you will never pray again'; that is, as though you see yourself as having never prayed. If such a one as this is called at the Reckoning, 'O you who neglected the prayer!', he will not argue on his own behalf that he did used to pray, because he will have been unaware of his own prayer and lost in the vision of Him to whom he prayed. Ibn ʿĀṭā' Allāh says in the *Ḥikam*, 'No act is more likely to be accepted than the one of which you are oblivious, and whose very existence you deem unlikely.' This is the prayer of one who bids farewell to his own prayer.

As for the one whose prayer is the focus of his attention and who relies on his prayer both outwardly and inwardly, he has not bade farewell to it. How could he possibly bid it farewell when he hopes to use it as an argument against God, as though reminding Him of the favour he did Him by performing it? Such a person's prayer does not ascend from him, because he is attached to it, *He raises the righteous deed* [Q.xxxv.10]. Had it truly been raised from him, he would have forgotten it and become oblivious to it, and it would be nothing to him. When something rises upwards, it shrinks in the eyes of those who behold it and becomes smaller and smaller until it disappears entirely. This is the understanding of the spiritual elite.

The third interpretation is the noblest one of all. It is held by those who, when they hear the word 'prayer' (*ṣalāt*), think immediately of the prayer of connection (*ittiṣāl*) known to the Sufis as enfolding (*ṭayy*), or we might say extinction (*fanā'*). Prayer is a connection (*waṣla*) between the servant and his Lord; when this connection is made, illusions disappear and multiplicity falls away in the blinding light of direct vision. For these people this is the only true prayer there is, because no other prayer makes this connection. The 'one who bids farewell' in their eyes in the one who says goodbye to all existence and breaks away from it and leaves it behind him, saying, *I have set my face toward Him who made the heavens and the earth, a man of primordial faith, and not an idolater* [Q.VI.79]. In this he has the best of examples. *Glory be to Him who took His servant by night...* [Q.XVII.1] until he *drew nigh, and came down, till He was but two bows' nigh, or nearer* [Q.LIII.8–9]. He cannot arrive until he first bids farewell to everything; after that, there is nothing to prevent the branch from connecting to the Root. At this point the intermediary disappears, and there is no need for a link or a base; when the subject is identical with the predicate, it requires no linking word: 'I am his hearing, his sight...'[1] This is the true prostration,[2] and such people accept no other.

As for the Prophet's words 'As though you will never pray again', it is just so, for their prayer (*ṣalāt*) are not disconnected [from each other]; their prostration is thus continuous. This is why it is said, 'Once they prostrated, they never rose again; once they arrived, they never returned.' *Those who are constant in their prayer* [Q.LXX.23]. This is the source of joy for the prophets and messengers; the Prophet (may God bless him and grant him peace) said, 'The joy of my soul is in the prayer.'

Lord, make such a prayer the joy of all our souls, and protect us outwardly and inwardly; You are the Best of protectors.

2

QUESTION: What is the meaning of the 'wrong' and 'evil' in the words of the Prophet (may God bless him and grant him peace), 'Glory be to You, I have wronged myself and done evil, so forgive me, for none can forgive sins but You'?

1 Sacred *ḥadīth*.
2 *Sujūd*: is the prostration at the end of each cycle of prayer (*rakʿa*).

ANSWER: The Prophet wronged his own self by not giving it the reverence it deserved at the beginning, when he did not know its position in God's sight. He had in fact been a prophet all along, as can be seen in what he said after his own reality had been revealed to him, 'I was a prophet when Adam was between water and clay.' After discovering his true state, he realised that he had not given himself his due and that he had treated himself less than perfectly. Therefore he said, by way of confessing, 'Glory be to You, I have wronged myself' by not acknowledging it. The same is the case for the words of his fellow prophet,[1] *Glory be to You, I have been a wrong-doer!* [Q.XXI.87]. He was saying, as it were, 'Lord, do not take me to task now that I have come to know my hidden reality, which is a ray of Your dazzling lights. Whenever I did evil to myself in this way by putting myself in a station lower than should have been, forgive me for this; for none can forgive sins but You.' He deemed that it was his obligation to see himself just as God saw him, and furthermore to have faith in his own message, as God says, *The messenger believes in what has been revealed to him from his Lord* [Q.II.285].

It was to this that God alluded when He said, *That God may forgive you your former and your latter sin* [Q.XLVIII.2]. The former sin was what we have just described, and the latter sin was anything of the sort that might have remained and come to the surface from time to time, according to the dictates of human nature and the rhythms of time. The Prophet (may God bless him and grant him peace) would speak of those times when he sensed that he was undervaluing his own station by referring to 'rust' (*rān*) on the heart. He said, 'Indeed my heart becomes veiled, and I ask forgiveness of God seventy times a day.'

God then says in the same verse, *and that He might complete his favour unto you*, that is, that He might never again veil you from what He revealed to you about yourself being one of the divine Realities; *and guide you to a straight path* and to the utmost end of the path until you reach a point where your reality is never veiled from you for

1 Jonah.

a moment; *and that God might help you with mighty help* against every misgiving that comes your way to upset your immersion in the vision of God Almighty.

3

QUESTION: What is the meaning of God's words as quoted by the Prophet (may God bless him and grant him peace): 'Call on Me (*udʿūnī*) with a tongue with which you have never disobeyed Me'?

ANSWER: The first thing that comes to mind when hearing this *ḥadīth* is that you should be kind to people so that they will pray to God for you with their tongues; when they pray for you, they do so with tongues with which you yourself have committed no sin.

What is more important than this—and God knows best—is that this is God's way of telling us to pray to Him with the supplications in the Holy Qur'ān, which will protect our prayers from error and made them more likely to be answered. The Qur'ān contains many prayers of the prophets (may God bless them and grant them peace), whose tongues were protected from error and who never asked the impossible of God. Thus God tells the supplicant not to pray with his own tongue, which has oft uttered lies and untruths. Moreover it is obvious that there is no prayer more comprehensive, eloquent or likely to be accepted than the likes of *Lord, You have given me dominion and taught me the interpretation of events. Maker of the heavens and the earth, You are my Patron in the herebelow and the hereafter. Cause me to die in surrender to You, and join me to the righteous!* [Q.XII.101]. When the supplicant recites such prayers, he will have more chance of an answer, and these prayers will not be made with his own tongue.

We have one more interpretation, which needs a little effort to understand. It is that one should not call upon God until one is near to Him and the Real has made one arrive to Him; and this arrival can only to confirmed when the Real is one's tongue. The Real only becomes one's tongue if one fulfils one's religious obligations and then draws nigh to Him with extra devotion until God's love for one is assured, whereupon the Real will become one's hearing, sight and tongue, as the *ḥadīth* says.[1] Once the Almighty Real has become one's limbs, one may then call upon Him, because one's tongue is now the tongue of God and not the same tongue it was before. God says, *If We willed, We could exchange their forms completely* [Q.LXXVI.28]. Then there will be nothing to stop one's prayer being answered. Before this point, it is not appropriate to engage in much supplication, since one is distant from God; and *God only accepts from those who are conscious of Him* [Q.V.27].

4

QUESTION: What is the meaning of the *ḥadīth* 'Your fathers will be better than your sons until the Day of Resurrection'? The *ḥadīth* seems to suggest that fathers will always be superior to sons until the end of time, yet reality says otherwise, as many sons obtain virtue which their fathers did not have.

ANSWER: This is a *ḥadīth* that has been passed around by both the masses and the elites, yet I do not know of anyone who has explained its meaning or shared their reflections on it. The fact is that it is too simple to pose any problems for an intelligent person, because the Prophet (may God bless him and grant him peace) did not say, 'Fathers will be better than sons', lest things be confused; what he said was '*Your* fathers will be better than *your* sons', i.e. your own personal fathers. This means that each individual person's father is better for him than his son. The Prophet knew that the soul naturally prefers the son to the father, but actually the father is better for a person than his son, both in worldly and religious affairs. When it comes to the life of this world, the father is better because he does not drive his son towards reckless behaviour as the son naturally does the father, *Your children and your wealth are a trial* [Q.LXIV.15]. When it comes to

1 Reference to the famous sacred *ḥadīth*; see above, page 13.

the hereafter, the father is better because the recompense one earns by being kind to his father is more than he earns from being kind to his son. This will remain true until the Day of Resurrection.

5

QUESTION: What is the nature of the comparison made in the invocation taught by the Prophet (may God bless him and grant him peace), 'God, bless Muḥammad and the family of Muḥammad as you blessed Abraham and the family of Abraham…'? When you compare one thing to another, the subject of the comparison is not as strong as the object; this would mean that the level of our master Abraham is higher than the level of our master Muḥammad (may God bless him and grant him peace), which is why the latter was asking God to make him like the former.

ANSWER: It seems to me that the comparison here is between the family of Muḥammad and the family of Abraham, which indeed would accord with the principle of the subject not being stronger than the object of comparison, since the family of Abraham had prophets and messengers among its numbers, including our own Prophet (may peace and blessings be upon them all).

If we wished to say more about the meaning of the *ḥadīth*, we would say that when the Prophet was told of the blessings God had sent upon him with His words, *Verily, God and His angels invoke blessings upon the Prophet* [Q.XXXIII.56], this verse said nothing about his family, and he yearned for his own family to be granted the same blessings as were granted to the family of Abraham. Therefore he encouraged the Companions to ask this of God, telling them to say, 'God, bless Muḥammad and the family of Muḥammad as you blessed Abraham and the family of Abraham.' In His grace, God answered this prayer and revealed words to suggest that His blessing had been granted to all the Prophet's community, not only his family and companions. He said, declaring his favour to this community,

He it is who invokes blessings upon you, as do His angels, to bring you forth from the shadows into the light [Q.XXXIII.43]. With this the favour was completed, praise be to God!

6

QUESTION: What is the meaning of the *ḥadīth* in the *Jāmiʿ al-Ṣaghīr*, 'The Jews divided into seventy-one sects, and the Christians divided into seventy-two sects, and my community will divide into seventy-three sects, all of whom will be in Hell save for one: the one I and my Companions follow.'

ANSWER: This *ḥadīth* would bring ruin to the Muḥammadan community if we were to understand it as most commentators have, because it seems to say that only one seventy-third of the Muḥammadan community will have salvation. Therefore what we hope from God—and what accords better with the compassion of the Prophet (may God bless him and grant him peace) with the believers—is that this *ḥadīth* is speaking of the community to whom the call is made (*ummat al-daʿwa*), not the community who answer the call (*ummat al-ijāba*); for the Prophet said, 'I am the messenger to those I meet alive and those born after me.' That the community meant here is the community to whom the call was given is supported by the Prophet's words, 'Whosoever dies ascribing no partners to God will enter Paradise,' and 'Whosoever's last words are *there is no god but God* will enter Paradise,' and God's words *God does not forgive that aught be associated with Him, but He forgives all besides that for whom He will* [Q.IV.48], and so on.

Now it is beyond doubt that the community who answered the call has not been deprived of its share of *tawḥīd* or acknowledgement of the Prophet's message. Though it has divided into branches, its root remains firm. The Prophet's intercession will encompass all who claim allegiance to him, whoever they might be; and one must always think the best of God.

It may be that the religions (*milal*)[1] before the coming of Moses (upon whom be peace) was seventy, and that the religion established by Moses was the seventy-first, and that all were Hell-bound except Moses and his followers. Then when God sent Jesus (upon whom be peace), this made seventy-two religions, all Hell-bound except that of Jesus and his followers. Then when God sent Muḥammad (may God bless him and grant him peace) with His compassionate Sacred Law, the number of sects became seventy-three, all Hell-bound except that of Muḥammad and his followers. They were all his community with respect to the call, as we have said. We should always think the best of God; and He is our sufficiency and the best of patrons.

7

QUESTION: What is the meaning of the *ḥadīth* 'People are asleep; when they die, they awaken.'

ANSWER: Indeed they are asleep. For example, the Companions (God be pleased with them) saw a man come to the Prophet (may God bless him and grant him peace) to ask him about the religion, and they had no idea that it was actually the angel Gabriel until the Prophet informed them of this, saying, 'That was Gabriel, who came to teach you your religion.' For he was awake while they were asleep. On another occasion he said, 'We prophets—our eyes sleep, but our hearts do not.'

1 *Milal* is the plural of *millat* and is most often used in the Qur'ān to refer to the religion of Abraham: II.130, II.135, III.95, etc. The Shaykh al-ʿAlawī here uses *milal* for the religions of the earlier prophets and the Sacred Law (*sharīʿa*) for the religion of the Prophet Muḥammad.

Appendix II

Arabic Text of Shaykh Muḥammad al-Ḥabīb's
Invocation of Blessings on the Prophet

اَللَّهُمَّ صَلِّ وَسَلِّمْ بِأَنْوَاعِ كَمَالَاتِكَ

فِي جَمِيعِ تَجَلِّيَاتِكَ عَلَى سَيِّدِنَا وَمَوْلَانَا مُحَمَّدٍ

أَوَّلِ الْأَنْوَارِ الْفَائِضَةِ مِنْ بَحْرِ عَظَمَةِ الذَّاتِ

الْمُتَحَقِّقِ فِي عَالَمَيِ الْبُطُونِ وَالظُّهُورِ بِمَعَانِي الْأَسْمَاءِ وَالصِّفَاتِ

فَهُوَ أَوَّلُ حَامِدٍ وَمُتَعَبِّدٍ بِأَنْوَاعِ الْعِبَادَاتِ وَالْقُرُبَاتِ

وَالْمُمِدِّ فِي عَالَمَيِ الْأَرْوَاحِ وَالْأَشْبَاحِ لِجَمِيعِ الْمَوْجُودَاتِ

وَعَلَى آلِهِ وَأَصْحَابِهِ صَلَاةً تَكْشِفُ لَنَا النِّقَابَ

عَنْ وَجْهِهِ الْكَرِيمِ فِي الْمَرَائِي وَالْيَقَظَاتِ

وَتُعَرِّفُنَا بِكَ وَبِهِ فِي جَمِيعِ الْمَرَاتِبِ وَالْحَضَرَاتِ

وَالْطُفْ بِنَا يَا مَوْلَانَا بِجَاهِهِ

فِي الْحَرَكَاتِ وَالسَّكَنَاتِ وَاللَّحَظَاتِ وَالْخَطَرَاتِ

سُبْحَانَ رَبِّكَ رَبِّ الْعِزَّةِ عَمَّا يَصِفُونَ

وَسَلَامٌ عَلَى الْمُرْسَلِينَ

وَالْحَمْدُ لِلَّهِ رَبِّ الْعَالَمِينَ

BIBLIOGRAPHY

Abdel Haleem, M. A. S. *The Qur'an: A New Translation*. Oxford: Oxford University Press, 2004.

ʿAlawī, Aḥmad al-. *Aʿdhab al-manāhil fī al-ajwiba wa'l-rasā'il*. Mostaghanem: al-Maṭbaʿa al-ʿAlāwiyya, 1993.

———. *Al-Baḥr al-masjūr fī tafsīr al-Qur'ān bi-maḥḍ al-nūr*. Mostaghanem: al-Maṭbaʿa al-ʿAlāwiyya, 1995.

———. *Dawḥat al-asrār fī maʿnā al-ṣalāt ʿalā al-nabī al-mukhtār*. Mostaghanem: al-Maṭbaʿa al-ʿAlāwiyya, 1991.

———. *Dīwān*. Beirut: Dār al-Kutub al-ʿIlmiyya, 2006.

———. *Lubāb al-ilm fī Sūrat wa'l-Najm*. Mostaghanem: al-Maṭbaʿa al-ʿAlāwiyya, n.d.

———. *Miftāḥ ʿulūm al-sirr fī tafsīr Sūrat al-ʿAṣr*. Mostaghanem: al-Maṭbaʿa al-ʿAlāwiyya, n.d.

Ali, Abdullah Yusuf. *The Meaning of the Holy Qur'an*. Beltsville: Amana Publications, 2004.

Asad, Muḥammad. *The Message of the Qur'an*. Gibraltar: Dar al-Andalus, 1984.

Baghdādī, ʿAbd al-Qāhir al-. *Al-Farq bayn al-firaq*. Beirut: Dār al-Āfāq al-Jadīda, 1971.

Burckhardt, Titus. *The Essential Titus Burckhardt*. Edited by William Stoddart. Bloomington: World Wisdom, 2003.

Cadavid, Leslie. *Two Who Attained: Twentieth Century Sufi Saints: Shaykh Ahmad al-Alawi and Fatima al-Yashrutiyya*. Louisville: Fons Vitae, 2005.

Chittick, William. *The Sufi Path of Knowledge: Ibn al-ʿArabi's Metaphysics of Imagination*. Albany: SUNY Press, 1989.

Hood, John (ed.). *The Essential Aquinas: Writings on Philosophy, Religion, and Society*. Westport: Praeger, 2002.

Ḥusaynī, Aḥmad ibn ʿAjība al-. *al-Futūḥāt al-Ilāhiyya*. Damascus: al-Yamāma, 1986.

Iskandarī, Ibn ʿAṭā Allāh al-. *The Book of Wisdom*. Translated by Victor Danner. New York: Paulist Press, 1978.

Lings, Martin. *The Holy Qur'ān: Translations of Selected Verses*. Cambridge: Royal Aal al-Bayt Institute for Islamic Thought & Islamic Texts Society, 2007.

———. *Muḥammad: his life based on the earliest sources*. Cambridge: Islamic Texts Society, 1994.

———. *A Return to the Spirit*. Louisville: Fons Vitae, 2005.

———. *A Sufi Saint of the Twentieth Century: Shaikh Aḥmad al-ʿAlawī his spiritual heritage and legacy*. Cambridge: Islamic Texts Society, 1993.

Nasr, Seyyed Hossein. *The Garden of Truth*. New York: Harper Collins, 2007.

Nicholson, Reynold. *Studies in Islamic Mysticism*. Cambridge: Cambridge University Press, 1921.

Pickthall, Marmaduke. *The Glorious Koran*. London: Fine Books and George Allen & Unwin, 1976.

Schuon, Frithjof. *Spiritual Perspectives and Human Facts*. London: Perennial Books, 1987.

———. *Understanding Islam*. Bloomington: World Wisdom, 1998.

Sirāj ad-Dīn, Abū Bakr. *The Book of Certainty*. Cambridge: Islamic Texts Society, 1992. Bibliography

INDEX